# READING KHALED HOSSEINI

# READING KHALED HOSSEINI

Rebecca Stuhr

The Pop Lit Book Club

**GREENWOOD PRESS**
*An Imprint of ABC-CLIO, LLC*

A B C 🔖 C L I O

Santa Barbara, California • Denver, Colorado • Oxford, England

**Library of Congress Cataloging-in-Publication Data**

Stuhr, Rebecca.
  Reading Khaled Hosseini / Rebecca Stuhr.
      p.   cm.   —   (The pop lit book club)
  Includes bibliographical references and index.
    ISBN 978-0-313-35511-0 (alk. paper) — ISBN 978-0-313-35512-7 (ebook)
1. Hosseini, Khaled. I. Title.
PS3608.O832Z87 2009
813'.6—dc22        2009026321

13   12   11   10   09   1   2   3   4   5

This book is also available on the World Wide Web as an eBook.
Visit www.abc-clio.com for details.

ABC-CLIO, LLC
130 Cremona Drive, P.O. Box 1911
Santa Barbara, California 93116-1911

This book is printed on acid-free paper (∞)

Manufactured in the United States of America

To the librarians and staff of the
Free Library of Philadelphia
in recognition of their hard work and dedication
to the young people of Philadelphia

# CONTENTS

# PREFACE

The purpose of this volume in the Pop Lit Book Club series is to introduce readers to the author Khaled Hosseini, his works, and their place in contemporary culture. Hosseini is a relatively new author. His first book, *The Kite Runner,* was published in 2003, and *A Thousand Splendid Suns* was published four years later in 2007. Both have enjoyed bestseller status and have been popular book club choices. Divided into nine chapters that examine Hosseini's novels from a variety of perspectives, this book should be a valuable resource for schoolteachers, librarians, and book club and reading group facilitators. It is also a resource for independent readers, both those who are approaching Hosseini for the first time and those who are familiar with his works but who are interested in a deeper look at the author and his novels.

The book begins with an overview of the author's life and ends with suggestions for further readings. The first chapter presents experiences from Hosseini's childhood in Afghanistan, to his immigration to the United States following the Communist coup in Kabul, through his education in American schools and universities to the launch of his writing career. Chapter 2 explores the structure of both novels. Although the plots of these novels are quite different one from another, the structures of these plots have shared elements. The chapter takes a close look at these elements and into the motivations that drive the characters to determine where these works of fiction can be placed within the complex genre that is the novel. Chapters 3 and 4 present a detailed look at the novels, providing for each novel an extensive plot summary, an analysis of the characters and settings, and a thorough examination of the themes.

In chapters 5 through 9, readers will find a variety of resources for learning more about Hosseini and his works, and explore popular and critical views of *The Kite Runner, A Thousand Splendid Suns*, and Hosseini himself. In chapter 5, the focus is on issues of contemporary importance as represented by the author. Chapter 6 looks at elements of popular culture appearing in Hosseini's novels and examines the impact his novels have had on current popular trends and culture. Additionally, this chapter looks at the film adaptation of *The Kite Runner.* Chapter 7 brings together and describes Web sites and other Internet resources, from Hosseini's official Web site, to podcasts featuring the author, to interactive fan sites that inform and entertain. Finally, in chapter 8, readers will find a review of the critical reception of *The Kite Runner* and *A Thousand Splendid Suns* found in the many reviews that have appeared in journals, magazines, newspapers, and radio and television broadcasts. Along with this, I provide a look at the media treatment of Hosseini as an author and individual, as well as Hosseini's public persona.

Chapter 9 concludes with suggestions for readers who are wondering what to read next. This annotated list includes contemporary and classic works of fiction, history and memoirs, short stories, and poetry. Whether one is approaching this selection in hopes of discovering a new favorite novel, or with the desire to learn more about the people, history, and culture of Afghanistan, "What Do I Read Next?" is an interesting and useful resource.

Following most chapters readers will discover a list of questions intended to stimulate discussion and to lead to a greater understanding of the author and his novels. In most of the chapters, readers will find sidebars that provide background and historical and social context to people, events, customs, and practices found in the pages of Hosseini's novels. A final Resources chapter brings together all of the sources that were consulted to write this book. Many of the citations include URLs that can be used to take curious readers directly to a particular online source.

My own experience in writing this book has led me to have a deep respect for Mr. Hosseini as both a writer and a humanitarian. Whether a devoted fan or someone with a passing interest in the writer and his works, my hope is that the materials within these pages make it possible to have a rich and informed engagement with the works of Khaled Hosseini.

I'd like to thank Grinnell College and the Grinnell College Libraries for making it possible for me to take the time necessary to write this book; Mark Schneider who supported my efforts in multiple tangible and intangible ways; the Swarthmore College Library, The Free Library of Philadelphia, Swarthmore Public Library, and, of course, Grinnell College Libraries for the use of their fine collections; my sister, Deborah Iwabuchi for her time and expert comments; editors George Butler and Kaitlin Ciarmiello at Greenwood Press for their generous and excellent guidance; Catherine, Jorge, Erma, Gretchen, and Tim, who are supportive beyond reason; and, finally, my beloved children and family, Martin, Helen, Bobbie, Wally, Philip, Yolanda, Victoria, Julian, PJ, Ikuo, Manna, and Hikari.

# KHALED HOSSEINI: A WRITER'S LIFE

The details available to us about Hosseini's life are significant and derive primarily from the many interviews in which he has participated since the publication and runaway success of *The Kite Runner*. The oldest of five children, Hosseini was born in Kabul in 1965. As noted at his official Web site, his mother taught Farsi and history at a girls' high school in Kabul. His father was a diplomat for Afghanistan's Foreign Ministry, and when he was posted to Afghanistan's embassy in Tehran, the family moved with him. The Hosseinis returned to Afghanistan in 1973, the year that King Zahir Shah was overthrown by Daoud Khan in a bloodless coup. From 1973 until 1976, Hosseini attended a French-styled high school in Kabul, the Istiqlal Lycee. In the same year, the family moved once again, this time to Paris, where his father took a new diplomatic post.

Hosseini's father was the second secretary to Afghanistan's ambassador in Paris, or the third-ranking diplomat serving there. During his assignment in Paris, the Hosseini family received news, through their government connections and friends in Afghanistan and from French news sources, of the Communist coup and then the Soviet invasion of Afghanistan. The Hosseinis heard stories of executions and learned of the deaths of friends and distant relatives and realized that they would not be able to return to Afghanistan. Hosseini told Terry Gross in a 2005 interview on her WHYY public radio program *Fresh Air* that when his father became aware that people connected with the ousted regime were in danger, he began secretly to arrange for political asylum for himself and his family in the United States. Hosseini told Gross that it would be hard to find an Afghan who did not have friends or relatives in Afghanistan who had been "executed, imprisoned, or harmed in some way" following the Communist coup. In 1980, the Hosseini family left Paris for a new life in San Jose, California, knowing that they might never return to Afghanistan. There they joined a growing San Francisco Bay Area Afghan community.

Hosseini attended high school in San Jose, graduating in 1984. He earned a degree in biology from Santa Clara College, and then went on to study medicine at the University of California, San Diego, completing his residency at Cedars-Sinai Hospital in Los Angeles. He practiced medicine as a primary care physician at a large health management organization (HMO) from 1996 to 2004. He is married and has two children: a son Haris and a daughter Farah. His wife Roya was born in Bethesda, Maryland, and is a lawyer. Hosseini returned to Kabul in 2003, spending two weeks visiting the sites of his childhood and traveling more widely to learn firsthand about the current conditions and outlook of the Afghan people. He was named as a Goodwill Envoy to the United Nations Refugee Agency (UNHCR) in 2006 and has returned to Afghanistan and traveled to refugee camps in Chad as part of his UN assignment.

Hosseini was interested in writing and storytelling from a young age. He told Tamara Jones of the *Washington Post* that he wrote plays as a child, "cajoling his younger brothers and cousins into performing" them. Later as an adult, he found writing a welcome change of pace from the hours he spent at his medical practice. Jones wrote, "[m]edicine was like an arranged marriage he grew fond of; writing was the grand romance between high school sweethearts" (Jones 2007). He told James Cowan of *National Post* that he started writing "suspense thrillers and Victorian tales of gothic horror, but soon moved on to short pieces of literary fiction" (Cowan 2003). Mir Tamim Ansary mentioned Hosseini in his

---

Zahir Shah was the king of Afghanistan from 1933 to 1973. He became king after the assassination of his father and was overthrown by his cousin Daoud Khan. Zahir Shah was out of the country at the time of the coup and he spent many years in exile in Italy. The current constitution of Afghanistan names Zahir Shah as The Father of the Nation. This title carries with it no political power and it cannot be transferred to an heir.

book *West of Kabul, East of New York* (2002) and described him as a "young Afghan doctor whose passion after work was writing—not *ghazals*, not *quasidas*, not even *rubaiyat*, but horror stories in the tradition of H.P. Lovecraft" (284).

Hosseini began writing for publication in 1999, and started working on *The Kite Runner* in 2001. This novel evolved from a short story begun two years earlier. It sat on a shelf in the garage until his wife found it and read it and then gave it to her father to read. Hosseini's father-in-law liked the story and told Hosseini that he wished it were longer. Hosseini wrote in a statement he prepared for Amazon.com that after looking at it again, he realized that it might work as a novel and began working on it that night. He continued to work on it, writing every morning between 5:00 A.M. and 8:00 A.M. before going to his medical practice. He was two-thirds of the way through the book when the September 11 attacks occurred. Hosseini considered abandoning the novel believing that with such dire news out of Afghanistan his depiction of his childhood Kabul would not resonate with a world that now saw Afghanistan as the "bad guys" (Jones 2007). He thought he might be content to write his novel for his family only, but his wife Roya suggested that he now had the opportunity to "put a human face on the Afghan people" (Hosseini, Amazon.com). With this encouragement, he went on to finish the book and seek publication.

In his 2006 dissertation on Afghan diasporic literary works, Mir Hekmatullah Sadat interviewed Hosseini. Hosseini told him that *The Kite Runner* began with a series of autobiographical episodes (164). But, he told Cowan that the novel is autobiographical only in "broad strokes . . . it is more fictional than most people realize." Like Amir and his father, Hosseini immigrated to the United States after the Soviet invasion. Both Baba and Hosseini's father were influential, had international careers, and lost everything as they sought refuge from the Communist takeover. The descriptions of Amir's childhood in Kabul are based on Hosseini's memories of his childhood there. Like Amir, a highlight of his childhood was the long winter vacation, kite flying, and kite fighting. In a 2003 interview with Razeshta Sethna in *Newsline*, Hosseini said that "I experienced Kabul with my brother the way Amir and Hassan do: long school days in the summer, kite fighting in the winter time, westerns with John Wayne at Cinema Park, big parties at our house in Wazir Akbar Khan, picnics in Paghman." He went on to say that unlike the generation of Afghans growing up in the twenty-first century, his memories are "untainted by the spectre of war, landmines, and famine." Other aspects of both *The Kite Runner* and *A Thousand Splendid Suns* are based on Hosseini's personal knowledge of and experience with Afghanistan during his childhood, and from his return visit in 2003. Jones wrote that his two-week visit "would provide much of the material for *A Thousand Splendid Suns*." Hosseini told her that "[t]o my knowledge, everything I wrote was based on something I saw or heard." But some of the things he saw there he was unable to write about. Hosseini told Jones that "some of the things were so cartoonishly heinous as to defy all comprehension."

Hosseini touches on the role of women in both of his novels, but it is the main theme of *A Thousand Splendid Suns*. He was raised at a time in Afghanistan when women were free to attend schools and seek professional employment. Many women in his family were professionals, and he was not raised with the worldview of protecting women from outside intrusion. He wrote in the BookBrowse interview that he hopes readers will develop a sense of empathy for Afghans and specifically for Afghan women, "on whom the effects of war and extremism have been devastating. I hope this novel brings depth, nuance, and emotional subtext to the familiar image of the *burqa*-clad woman walking down a dusty street." He continued, asserting that under the Taliban,

> women were denied education, the right to work, the right to move freely, access to adequate healthcare, etc. Yet I want to distance myself from the notion, popular in some circles, that the West can and should exert pressure on these countries to grant women equal rights. . . . This approach either directly or indirectly dismisses the complexities and nuances of the target society as dictated by its culture, traditions, customs, political system, social structure, and overriding faith. (BookBrowse 2007)

Hosseini told Jones that he has received criticism for having portrayed women who wear and come to terms with the *burqa*. Both of his main female characters in *A Thousand Splendid Suns* at some point, as they are out in the streets clad in the garment, express a satisfaction with the anonymity and sense of protection they feel from wearing it. Hosseini claims no sympathy for this practice, and states that he wishes "every single woman in Afghanistan could lift the *burqa* and walk the streets freely," but he also believes that this should be a choice that the women make. He points out that women wore them in Afghanistan for centuries before the Taliban came to power. "It is not quite the concern for women in Afghanistan as it is for us in the West. It's not as urgent a matter as security, as food, as being able to get medical care for their kids. I'm just not sure," Hosseini continued, "what a reliable gauge of women's liberation in Afghanistan the burqa is" (Jones 2007).

Hosseini has received responses to his books from both Afghan and non-Afghan readers. He has received positive responses from most Afghan readers who feel "a slice of their story has been told by one of their own" (Sethna 2003). He has also heard from those who think that his writing is divisive. He is quoted in many interviews, including that of Sadat, as saying that those who found the book divisive objected to his bringing up issues of discrimination, racism, and ethnic inequality. But Hosseini has responded to them by saying that he believes these issues are important and should not be taboo. In fact, it is the role of fiction to take on these difficult subjects and open them up for debate (Sadat 2006, 166). He added in his interview with Sethna, "If this book generates any sort of dialogue among Afghans, then I think it will have done a service to the community" (2003). Non-Afghan readers have responded to the themes of friendship, betrayal, guilt, and redemption found in Western literary fiction. Hosseini wants readers to respond to his work as literature and storytelling; he also hopes that "the novel has provided Western readers with a fresh perspective." He laments the fact that stories from Afghanistan "center around the various wars, the opium trade, and the war on terrorism. Precious little is said about the Afghan people themselves, their culture, their traditions, how they lived in their country and how they manage abroad as exiles" (Azad 2004). Hosseini considers himself to be a storyteller using both the elements of literary fiction and genre writing. In his interview with Azad in afghan-magazine.com, Hosseini said that *The Kite Runner* was not influenced by Afghan literature. He elaborated further, describing his style of writing as "rooted in a western style of writing prose." However, he added,

> Afghanistan is full of great storytellers, and I was raised around people who were very adept at capturing an audience's attention with their storytelling skills. I have been told that there is an old fashioned sense of storytelling in *The Kite Runner*. I would agree. It's what I like to read, and what I like to write. (Azad 2004)

He told Jones that his writing is "spare, direct. My natural knack is for telling a story."

As a child, Hosseini read classical Dari poetry and some Western fiction translated into Farsi, including Mickey Spillane and *Alice in Wonderland*. Like his character Amir in *The Kite Runner*, Hosseini loved westerns as a child and his favorite film was *The Magnificent Seven* (Hansen 2003). He did not learn to read English until he moved to the

> Dari is the Farsi or Persian dialect of Afghanistan spoken by the Tajiks, Hazara, and Farsiwan. The Uzbeks and Turkmen speak Turkic dialects; Pashtuns speak Pashtu or Pashto. Dari is one of forty languages and dialects spoken in Afghanistan and it is one of the country's two official languages, with the second being Pashto. Uzbek, Turkmen, Balochi, Pashai, Nuristani, and Pamiri are all official third languages as of the 2004 constitution. (See Ludwig Adamec, *Historical Dictionary of Afghanistan*, and Kathryn M. Coughlin, *Muslim Cultures Today: A Reference Guide*.)

United States. He has said that the first book that he read and fully understood was Steinbeck's *Grapes of Wrath*. "Some of [what Steinbeck's characters experienced] reminded me of Afghans and what they had gone through, and even my own family to some extent" (Weich 2007). He noted in his interview with Azad that being an indigenous writer gives his writing authenticity. "[I]f you write with honesty and integrity, then it may show on the pages" (Azad 2004). Hosseni is quoted as saying that he does his best to "represent a view that is culturally accurate and historically legitimate. . . . Good stories must ring true, and for me, it always goes back to story" (Sadat 165). Hosseini feels comfortable writing about what he knows. He lived through the final years of the monarchy, the formation of the republic, and the early years of Daoud Khan's leadership. The Taliban portions of his books are taken from stories he heard directly from Afghans who were in Afghanistan during the Taliban years but who now live in the United States. He also relied on the media. He writes, "To my knowledge, everything I wrote was based on something I saw or heard" (Jones 2007). Still, he mentioned in the interview at BookBrowse, he feels that "it is quite a burden for a writer to feel a responsibility to represent his or her own culture and to educate others about it."

Hosseini writes that through Amir he represents important aspects of the Afghan immigrant, aspects that he himself shares. In particular, he mentions *The Kite Runner* protagonist Amir's longing and nostalgia for his homeland. In his depiction of Amir's childhood, Hosseini brings to life his own vivid memories of Kabul during the 1960s and 1970s, a period of time he refers to as a "Golden Era of sorts" (Azad 2004). Amir assimilates into American society, graduating from high school and attending college and beginning his career as a writer. His view of *nang* and *namoos* (the Afghan sense of honor and pride especially with regard to wives and daughters), as evidenced by his reaction to Soraya's pre-engagement confession, is softened not only by the guilt that he carries with him, but also by his exposure to different ideas and practices in the new country. After his father dies, Amir sells the van and stops attending the flea market, the social site of the Afghan community in the East Bay. Still, he marries an Afghan woman and relies on his connections with the extended Afghan community to bring Sohrab safely into the United States. This sense of belonging to the closely knit Afghan community can be attributed to Hosseini as well. He told Sadat that "after 25 years in the United States" he considers himself to be assimilated into American culture (Sadat, 164). He married an American-born Afghan woman, and he has raised his children to be bilingual. Hosseini told Terry Gross that maintaining the language is the most important way to preserve the culture and that food follows in importance. He and others in the Afghan community continue to practice traditional wedding celebrations, and the observation of Ramadan and its three days of feasts.

Although Amir's guilt is much more related to specific sins of commission and omission than what Hosseini describes as the survivor's guilt that he and other diasporic Afghans experience, it may be the inspiration for Amir's burden of memory. Hosseini described this lingering cloud that "many of us, particularly in sunny California, have felt at one time or another" (Azad 2004). He told Terry Gross that he carries an "undercurrent of guilt" about his own good fortunes and life. He thinks about people in Afghanistan who were poor and worked as cooks and gardeners, perhaps in his household, and he wonders how they have fared through the past twenty-five years of upheaval and bloodshed.

---

President Daoud was president of the Republic of Afghanistan from 1973 until 1978 when he was assassinated. Daoud came to power via a coup, which he staged. There was little resistance. Afghanistan was proclaimed a republic and a central committee was formed. This committee elected Daoud as president, prime minister, minster of foreign affairs, and minster of defense of the Republic of Afghanistan. Preceding this, Daoud had a long career in the military and in the political system of Afghanistan. As prime minister (1953–1963) he sought emancipation for women, encouraging them to give up the veil and to join the work force. The coup staged by the People's Democratic Party of Afghanistan (PDPA) on April 27, 1978, led to Daoud's assassination and brought Marxist rule to Afghanistan. (See Amin Saikal, et al., *Modern Afghanistan: A History of Struggle and Survival*, and Ludwig Adamec, *Historical Dictionary of Afghanistan*.)

The Afghan diaspora began in the 1970s with the advent of drought and famine. In these initial decades most Afghans leaving the country went to Pakistan or Iran. Later immigrants went to Western Europe and the United States. The largest populations in Europe are in Germany and the Netherlands with an estimated 200,000 in all of Europe and another 50,000 in the Russian Federation. Afghans began immigrating to the United States in the 1980s, moving through Pakistan and Germany. There are around 300,000 Afghans in North America with the highest concentration living in the San Francisco East Bay. Sadat writes that the city of Fremont is known as "Little Kabul." Afghan communities have also formed in Virginia, North Carolina, New Jersey, and Orange County, California. In 1980 there were about 500 Afghan families in the United States. By the year 2000, there were nearly 38,000 families. (See Mir Hekmatullah Sadat, "The Afghan Experience," and Eden Naby, "The Afghan Diaspora.")

Hosseini's *The Kite Runner* was released as a film directed by Marc Forster during the winter of 2008. The film sparked controversy when the young actors received death threats due to their participation in the rape scene. Both they and their families were relocated before the film was released. Hosseini told Erika Milvy of *Salon* in a December 9, 2007 interview, that this scene was pivotal to the integrity of the film. He expressed surprise that there could be a suggestion that this scene somehow condoned rape: "How anybody can see this film and walk away with the conclusion that it supports rape is unfathomable to me. This is a film that denounces what happened in that alley, not one that endorses it" (Milvy 2007). He concluded his interview with Milvy by pointing out that the film is about what is good in human nature.

> I hope this controversy hasn't overshadowed the fact that this is a film about good things—about the virtues of tolerance, friendship, brotherhood and love and harmony—and that it speaks against violence. There's a lovely scene in the film where Amir, in a moment of distress and personal anguish, goes to a mosque and prays. How many times have we seen Muslim characters in a film pray—in that kind of very spiritual moment, piously? Usually when they do, in the next scene they're blowing something up. And I'm proud of the fact that Muslims around the world will see this character performing this ritual exactly in the way that it was meant to be performed. (2)

IMDb (Internet Movie Database) and other sources note that a film version of *A Thousand Splendid Suns* is due out in 2009, written and directed by Stephen Zaillian and to be released by Columbia (see http://www.imdb.com/title/tt0959353/; http://www.comingsoon.net/films.php?id=37415). Hosseini told Milvy that he believes the film based on this novel, despite its violence and cruelty, will be "more palatable. There are issues [addressed in the book] about women, but the issues about ethnic tension are the sensitive ones in Afghanistan. If that film is ever made, I don't think we'll be facing the same sort of controversy" (Milvy 2007).

## DISCUSSION QUESTIONS

- Hosseini expresses concern about the burden writers have to represent their culture and to educate others about it. What barriers do you imagine ethnic or multicultural writers face with publishers or the reading public in writing beyond their personal experience or about communities other than their own? How might this compare to an American of white, European descent writing about communities and subjects beyond his or her immediate personal experience?

- Hosseini has a unique perspective as an Afghan and an American and a fluent speaker of both Dari and English. What strengths do these characteristics bring to his novels and how does knowing this about the author affect your reaction to Hosseini's work?

- Hosseini has said that medicine was like a good arranged marriage, but that writing was his grand romance. Imagine the discipline necessary to dedicate time to writing while pursuing a full-time career in a demanding field. What insight into Hosseini's personality does this give you and does it shed light on his choice of topics or style of writing?

# 2

# KHALED HOSSEINI AND THE NOVEL

Both of Khaled Hosseini's novels, *A Thousand Splendid Suns* and *The Kite Runner,* fit solidly within the Anglo-European literary tradition of the novel. The novel can be defined simply as an extended fictional account of the day-to-day events, tragic and comic, of everyday human beings. Within this broad definition of the novel, a fluid number of terms are used to describe subcategories, some of which include The *bildungsroman* (the novel of transformation) and its close cousin the *künstlerroman* (the development of the artist), and the historical novel (in the tradition of Sir Walter Scott and Leo Tolstoy). Other subcategories include the novel of immigration, the ethnic novel, diasporic fiction, the autobiographical novel (for instance *What Is the What* by Dave Eggers), and the novel of manners, and domestic fiction (often attributed to Jane Austen and Charles Dickens). Other possible subcategories or genres within the novel tradition include experimental fiction, science fiction, romance fiction, the detective novel, the mystery novel, young adult fiction, and urban street fiction. Narrative styles include stream-of-consciousness (James Joyce, William Faulkner, William Styron), first-person narrative, the omniscient narrator, and combinations of the above. These descriptive terms are so fluid with varying and sometimes controversial definitions because a mythic or archetypal structure to the novel follows the everyday occurrences of the common person: issues of birth, death, love, hate, loss, and triumph. The novel was "novel" or new because the protagonist or hero was the common person as opposed to the near-godly hero of the epic poem. It is possible to apply one or more of these descriptive terms or forms to Hosseini's novels beginning with *bildungsroman* and ending with domestic and literary fiction.

## FORMS OF THE NOVEL THAT CAN BE USED TO DESCRIBE *THE KITE RUNNER* AND *A THOUSAND SPLENDID SUNS*

The *bildungsroman,* or novel of transformation, follows the life of the young man or woman as they become aware of the limitations imposed upon them by family and the inadequacy of their education opportunities. The protagonist in the *bildungsroman* breaks away, leaving behind family and town to find freedom and new opportunities in a new environment. The central character in this novel of transformation would not have to be, but generally is, a member of the middle class or perhaps the lower classes. It is important to the plot of the *bildungsroman* that the main character is somehow constrained, breaks the constraining bonds, goes elsewhere to learn and discover him or herself, finds freedom or emancipation, and returns home.

In the domestic fiction of Jane Austen and Charles Dickens, the family may be the center of the activities and most, although not all, of the action takes place in the setting of the home: the drawing room, the ballroom, the kitchen, the study, or sleeping quarters. Servants, characters on the street, and the commercial realm figure into these stories, but the main characters are brothers and sisters, husbands and wives, mothers, and fathers, and their children (whether or not they own the house or work in the house).

The historical novel has elements of real people and actual events, but these people and events are settings within which the central characters of the novel are placed. The autobiographical novel similarly may be substantially based on the life of the author, but with enough fabrication or deviation from the basic facts to warrant calling it a novel rather than an autobiography. Finally, the ethnic or diasporic novel, or novel of immigration, are labels often used to describe novels written by authors who are from a diasporic or immigrant group, including European ethnicities. The author does not necessarily choose to have his or her works labeled or categorized in this way. Authors may consider such a categorization to be empowering or to diminish their work—relegating it to a subcategory of literature, whereas the work of white authors simply is considered to be "literature." Publishers, though, may classify a novel in this way because they believe it will help sales.

The novel of immigration is a classification that can be applied to European immigrant writers of the nineteenth and early twentieth century, or to writers from the contemporary waves of immigration. Novelists who find themselves classified as ethnic novelists are often first- or second-generation Americans. Their novels may be or may appear to be autobiographical, or they may at least deal in a significant way with ethnic communities and individuals who are seeking to establish a unique and meaningful identity and to be recognized and respected within the dominant population and culture. The dominant culture, of course, is shifting and changing as it absorbs and reflects new cultures with which it comes into contact. And so it evolves into something that is in truth all encompassing.

## HOSSEINI AND STORYTELLING

Hosseini places his novels into the category of storytelling. He often refers to himself as a storyteller. He may simply say this out of humility, choosing not to attribute higher literary motives to his writing. He, however, does mention in more than one interview that there are many good storytellers in Afghanistan and that he grew up listening to stories. He thus separates himself and his writing in part from the Western novel tradition and links himself instead to a tradition that is part of the greater Afghan culture, or an oral tradition (Afghanistan also has a rich written poetry heritage). The novel as we know it has its roots in England and Western Europe. Daniel Defoe's *Robinson Crusoe* is considered to be the first English language novel, although, appearing centuries earlier, Petronius's first-century literary work, *The Satyricon,* has also been described as the earliest example of the novel. The form went through enormous development and experimentation even in the early decades of its appearance as an English language genre with the epistolary novels of Samuel Richardson and the quirky prenatal narration and typographical hijinks of Laurence Sterne's *Tristram Shandy.* Knowing that Hosseini's own early reading interests were solidly within the realm of Western literature, we can look at the various forms and styles associated with the novel, the *bildungsroman,* the historical novel, and even that of domestic fiction, as homes in which to place *The Kite Runner* and *A Thousand Splendid Suns.*

Ray Conlogue, in a 2003 article about Hosseini, writes,

> Hosseini is not an admirer of the kind of self-conscious and artful fiction so admired in Western countries. "Don't draw me into that," he says, laughing. "I'm not a big fan of hard-core literary fiction. I like stories. I grew up with stories, and stories

are all I can write. I can't write an amorphous plot." Nor does
he want to: He believes storytelling is more important. "And
the art of storytelling is endangered." (R1)

Storytelling, however, is an oral tradition. John Harrell writes in his 1983
book that the origins of story are in oral transmission, whether passing on
stories learned as a child or forming tales from one's own life or imagination. He cautions the would-be storyteller, "once an oral tradition is written down it ceases to be the one thing and becomes another" (29). He goes
on to say that literate persons are unable to carry on the oral tradition of
storytelling. "Literacy, with the sophistication that accompanies it, brings
into play wholly alien criteria that affect one's telling. . . . We never
belonged to [this tradition] in the first place, and we cannot reenter it"
(61–62).

Elie Wiesel, who refers to himself as a storyteller, is another writer
who relies on his own experiences and the history of his people for his
novels. He makes use of religious and folk texts and sees himself as continuing the Jewish tradition of storytelling as an oral and a textual practice. In her 2006 book on Wiesel, Rosemary Horowitz emphasizes his
role as a storyteller. She writes that Wiesel claims "the only role that
suits him is the one, less presumptuous . . . of the storyteller who transmits what was given to him, as faithfully as possible" (8). Horowitz
describes the storyteller as one who "does nothing but tell the tale: he
transmits what he has received, he returns what was entrusted to him.
His story does not begin with his own, it is fitted into the memory that
is the living tradition of his people" (9).

Hosseini may very well have approached the writing of his two novels from the point of view of a storyteller but, nonetheless, both novels
can be described as falling into one or more of the categories of literary
fiction described above. We can honor Hosseini's wish to be seen as a
storyteller and we can see that he fulfills some of that role by passing on
stories and experiences both from his own experience and from his
imagination. His narratives are straightforward tales centered on the
daily events of his protagonists. But, we can also enrich our own understanding of Hosseini's fiction by looking at it within the tradition of
Western literary fiction.

## HOSSEINI'S NOVELS AND THE EPIC TRADITION

In his 1995 book *Telling Stories: Postmodernism and the Invalidation of
Traditional Narrative,* Michael Roemer specifies a number of elements

present in stories whatever form they may take. These elements come out of the epic tradition: the hero and the quest. Roemer notes that the story is always set in the past, the central figure must act, these actions are often imposed rather than taken up by choice, and the outcome of these actions may not be what the hero intends. Beset by a crisis, the hero must seek to resolve it without the luxury of waiting for time or a logical progression of steps to aid in the resolution of the crisis. The hero and other characters in the story are constrained by their context: the time and place of their existence and the story evolves out of a situation that is already in place as the story unfolds to the reader or audience. Roemer explains that they are tied to their particular context and there is no escape (1995, 29, 35).

Certainly all of these elements described as being central to the epic are present in both of Hosseini's novels. In each novel, we have two protagonists, one growing up with a sense of entitlement and privilege and the other growing up under conditions circumscribed by poverty and social expectation. In *The Kite Runner,* Amir is suddenly thrown back to his childhood when he receives a phone call. After years of struggling with a guilty conscience and a lifetime of finding a place for himself within a family and society in which he has not quite measured up to the status and expectations of his father, he is given a task or quest, a quest that will "make him good again." While Amir has left the country, completed his education, and successfully launched his career as a writer (literate not only in his native Dari but also in his new language, English), Hassan has learned to read and write and has established a family. In the midst of his new life, Hassan is called on to return to his servant life and to protect Amir's family home. This is his task, and, born into a class that has been restricted to positions of servitude, he accepts this task, taking it out of a sense of loyalty to his former masters. Neither Amir nor Hassan is aware of the risks they will confront, nor do they set out with the expectation of sacrificing their lives to their task. Yet, this is what is asked of them. Hassan defiantly puts himself in the way of danger, and ultimately loses his life and the life of his wife for the sake of the household of Baba and Amir. Realizing this, Amir reluctantly sets out on his quest to rescue Hassan's son, Sohrab, to honor Hassan's loyalty and to absolve himself of guilt. Unlike Hassan, Amir is fortunate and survives to accomplish his task.

In Hosseini's second novel, Laila and Mariam's fates are connected through a tragic twist of circumstances. However, because of the status of women within the society, their decisions are made for them. Mariam must marry Rasheed because her father and his wives force her to do so. Her acceptance is merely a token act. Laila must marry Rasheed because she is orphaned and pregnant. Both situations are untenable in her society. Furthermore women may not travel alone or work and thus, should Laila choose any other course, even if she were not pregnant, her chances of survival would be slim. Together, Laila and Mariam must survive their marriage to a brutal and controlling man and protect the children. In the end, Mariam faces a crisis. She must kill Rasheed or allow Laila to be killed. She cannot wait to make a decision and calculate the costs; she must act immediately. Later, when she has time to consider the consequences of her action, she makes a carefully considered decision and then takes the steps necessary to fulfill it. Mariam, like Hassan, loses her life for the sake of her friend. Though she is not Laila's servant, unlike Laila, Mariam cannot envision a life different from the one she has been living. She is aware of having made life-changing decisions, and this is one more such decision. This time it is made in the interests of others, however, rather than out of self-interest. Laila, brought up to imagine a future, cannot imagine that Mariam is planning to give up her life, but in the end, she accepts Mariam's sacrifice and lives, as closely as she can, the life that Mariam envisioned for her.

Both *A Thousand Splendid Suns* and *The Kite Runner* end on mixed notes. The chance of happiness is evident, but the characters have so much to overcome to reach that happiness. For Amir, his happiness is tied up in Sohrab's well-being. Sohrab's wounds are deep and the healing process is slow. Laila, with her new life with Tariq and the children, has all the promise of happiness, but the society—the same one that separated her from Tariq and that took from her Mariam, her brothers, her mother, her father, and her home—has all the same oppressive and violent elements waiting to resurface and she can have no real sense of safety.

## HOSSEINI'S NOVELS AS *BILDUNGSROMAN*

The basic story elements surviving from the epic tale are also present in the *bildungsroman*. The *bildungsroman*, however, has as a focal point the development of the main character from childhood to maturity of mind and body. To gain this maturity, the character must leave home and family, learn about him- or her self through the experiences that life provides, rather than through formal schooling, and then return with newly acquired wisdom. In his book *Season of Youth: The Bildungsroman from Dickens to Golding* (1974), Jerome Buckley describes the *bildungsroman* as being the story of a sensitive child growing up with the pressure of social and intellectual constraints imposed on him or her by family or society. Finding schooling inadequate, the child eventually leaves home and, in many cases, leaves the countryside for the city to become independent. The life experiences of the child constitute his or her serious education. Buckley adds that the character must have "at least two love affairs or sexual encounters, one debasing, one exalting, and demands that in this respect and others the hero reappraise his values" (17–18). By the time the character has gone through these affairs and life experiences, he or she has left childhood and adolescence behind to reach adulthood. The character then returns home. Pin-chia Feng, in *The Female Bildungsroman by Toni Morrison and Maxine Hong Kingston: A Postmodern Reading* (1998), summarizes *bildungsroman* as traditional historic literature derived from the quest, with the protagonist moving toward the completion of his or her quest (2). Feng quotes Wilhelm Dilthey as describing the genre as representing the regular course of development in the life of an individual. Each stage in the life of the individual has value and moves him or her along to the next stage of life. Feng finds that sexuality for the female protagonist in a *bildungsroman* is "more often debasing and handicapping than exalting" (7) and that women find it more difficult to leave their family behind than the male characters (8). They are even more constrained by their social environments. Feng goes on to quote Bonnie Hoover Braendlin to explain that the feminist *bildungsroman* places the emphasis on "repressive environmental factors, on the process of disillusionment for personality change and maturity, and on the possibilities for transformation offered by individual choices," which lead to "female awakening and consciousness-raising and on proclaiming new, self-defined identities" (9).

As we think about these descriptions of *bildungsroman,* it becomes evident how both of Hosseini's novels fit into this rubric. Each novel is a dual *bildungsroman*. As stated earlier, each novel features two protagonists, one privileged and the other constrained by poverty and low status within the stratification of society. All four characters face an exile from their home. In this case, none of the four characters leave their home by choice. In *The Kite Runner,* Amir must leave with his father in the wake of the Soviet invasion, but this departure allows him to leave his past behind him and indirectly gives him a chance to begin anew. He is able to follow his own interests and ambitions in a new culture more friendly to his ambitions and to renew his relationship with his father. Amir and Baba are set on more of an equal footing as his father loses his status in the new country (although not within the Afghan community that has formed in that new country) and Amir is better than his father at negotiating the new language and customs. Hassan leaves the compound of Baba and Amir, forced out through Amir's jealousy, guilt, and deceit. He leaves with his father for their ethnic homeland, Hazarajat, where presumably they may live on an equal footing with other Hazaras, not in servitude as they do in a Pashtun-dominated city. Hassan's life continues without the reader, but we hear about it in retrospect after Taliban soldiers have killed both Hassan and his wife. Hassan is killed protecting Amir and Baba's house and grounds, and Hassan's wife is killed as she protects Hassan. They leave behind a child whose rescue becomes the object of Amir's quest.

In *A Thousand Splendid Suns,* Laila, neglected by her mother but nurtured and loved by her father, is forced out of her family after the death of her brothers and then the deaths of her mother and father. She only travels down the street, but it is as though she has arrived at another time and place. She goes from the child who plays in the streets, attends school, and has hopes and expectations for her future, to the wife of a man many decades her senior, confined to her home, and soon to be a mother. Mariam lives at home with her mother until she is fifteen. At that age, she walks the short distance from her small rural home to Herat to find her father. Once there, she learns for the first time that she is unwanted. This is what her mother has been telling her, but Mariam has never believed it. When she returns to her house, she finds that her mother has committed suicide. Although she is taken back to her father's house, she is then forcibly ejected by him and forced to marry Rasheed, the same man who later will marry Laila. With Rasheed, she travels to the much bigger city of Kabul. After a brief time of happiness with Rasheed, she loses favor and is reduced to a role that is more servant than wife.

As Mariam and Laila become closer through their shared love of Aziza, Laila's daughter, and a common need to survive the brutal and tyrannical Rasheed, Mariam, for the first time, finds herself wanted and needed and part of a family. By virtue of this sense of belonging, she undergoes a transformation that is complete at the point she tells Laila to "[t]hink like a mother. I am." After killing Rasheed to prevent him from killing Laila, Mariam, older and more accustomed to hardship, must form a plan to save them from the repercussions of her act. There is no possibility of convincing Talib authorities that she committed this act in self-defense. For women under the Taliban there is no self-defense, there is only obedience to the male authority, and punishment for failing to be obedient. Mariam, confident and in control, makes her decision to turn herself in. She is a mother sacrificing herself for her children. Laila, still young and still finding her way, cannot comprehend this decision, but follows Mariam's orders. Eventually, after returning to normalcy and an equal and loving relationship with Tariq and her two children, Laila makes the decision for her family to return to Kabul to help rebuild Afghanistan. She is pregnant again, and she and Tariq work with the Kabul orphanage to take care of the grounds and care for the orphans.

Returning to *The Kite Runner*, Amir, safely situated in the United States, has become closer to his father and they are part of a close-knit Afghan community. Amir continues to feel intense shame over his betrayal of Hassan. He is unable to tell his story to Soraya who has trusted Amir with her own story of shame. But through his relationship to Soraya and with her support, he follows his dream of becoming a writer and succeeds in publishing his first novel. They both break away from the constraining ties of their families and cultures. Soraya does so by pursuing her dream of becoming a teacher despite her father's desire that she choose a more auspicious career, perhaps returning to help rebuild Afghanistan. Amir chooses to be a writer rather than choosing a profession more acceptable to his father. He and Soraya move across the bay to San Francisco and are childless. Amir sees their childlessness as a curse arising from his mistreatment of Hassan.

His quest or challenge is presented to him in the form of a phone call from Rahim Khan, his mentor and his father's best friend, asking him to come to Pakistan, where Rahim now lives, and offering him the opportunity to "be good again." Unlike Mariam who came firmly and unswervingly to her decision to save Laila and her children, with her two-word sentence, "I am," conveying her strength and determination, Amir continues to make excuses as to why he cannot fulfill the task set before him by Rahim. As Rahim tries to convince Amir to go, Amir comes up with one excuse after another, even after he has heard how Hassan and his wife died protecting his property with no other compulsion but loyalty and a sense of duty. "Why me? Why can't you pay someone here to go? I'll pay for it if it's a matter of money." Insulted, Rahim is angry with Amir for perhaps the first time in his life. "[W]hy you? I think we both know why it has to be you, don't we?" (222–223). For the first time Amir realizes his secret is not his own, but, still unwilling to take on the task of rescuing Sohrab, Amir claims that he is unfit for the task. Just as his father had once predicted, he has become "a man who can't stand up to anything" (223). However, given some time to think about Hassan and the cycle of "lies, betrayals, and secrets" (226), Amir comes to a full recognition of Hassan's unfailing love for him and, despite his fear and reluctance, Amir decides to go to Kabul and rescue Sohrab, Hassan's son, and so his quest begins.

It is through this quest that Amir reaches his full maturity. On the quest, Amir is nearly beaten to death by his old nemesis, saved by Sohrab in a way that mirrors Hassan's own bravery and quick thinking, and after more missteps and hesitation, returns successfully to the United States with Sohrab. Amir has moved beyond himself to think first and foremost of Sohrab. He has more time than Mariam, more resources to call on to help him complete his task, the accomplishment of which leads him to his transformation.

Hassan's transformation takes place away from the reader. Loved by his father (unlike Mariam), he is loved and wanted despite his illegitimate birth and nurtured as a child despite all hardships. He marries and has his own loving family. He even welcomes back the mother who abandoned him at birth and brings her into the fold of his family. When Ali decides that he can only save Hassan by taking him away from the household they have served their entire lives, he provides the means for Hassan's transformation into a mature adult. Once away from the constraints of his servitude, Hassan flourishes. Significantly, he learns to read and makes sure that his own child is able to read.

## HISTORICAL NOVELS AND DOMESTIC FICTION

Because of these journeys of transformation undertaken by Amir, Hassan, Laila, and Mariam, it seems proper to describe Hosseini's two novels as *bildungsromane*. But both novels can be called historical novels as well because the reader learns so much about the history, culture, and customs of Afghanistan. This is especially true in *A Thousand Splendid Suns*, which takes place over several decades, predating the Soviet occupation and continuing into the U.S. invasion and occupation. In both novels, historical events and historical figures enter into the story. We can also view both novels as domestic fiction, although it is difficult to compare Hosseini's works with those of Austen because of the brutal nature of *A Thousand Splendid Suns* and the twentieth-century graphic reality of both novels. Both novels deal primarily with the intimate relationships of the family within the confines of the family home. Dickens may be a better author with whom to compare Hosseini, as he was much more likely than Austen to let the events of the outside world seep in to his tales and to deal with the seedier, more brutal side of everyday life. Finally, we cannot ignore the fact that Hosseini, the author, is an immigrant and a member of a minority group within the United States.

## THE NOVEL OF IMMIGRATION

Hosseini is an American and considers himself to have assimilated into U.S. culture. But his novels are centered on his ancestral and natal home and illuminate that home country, by providing a broader picture of

Hosseini mentions and quotes from many singers and poets in *A Thousand Splendid Suns.*

*Ustad Mohammad Hussain Sarahang* (1924–1983) was a famous Tajik classical musician from Afghanistan and known throughout Pakistan, India, and Iran. He was awarded the title Sarahang by the government of Afghanistan.

*Ustad Awal Mir* (also Awalmir) was a Pashtun singer. One of his most popular songs was "Da Zamong Zeba Watan, Da Zamong Laila Watan" (This Is Our Beautiful Country, This Is Our Dear Country), which was recorded in the 1970s.

*Hafez* (also Hafiz) was a poet from fourteenth-century Shiraz, now the capital of Fars Province in Iran. He is revered in Afghanistan and his poetry is considered to be divinely inspired.

*Ustad Khalilullah Khalili* (also Khalil Allah Khalili) is one of Afghanistan's foremost twentieth-century poets. He was born in 1908 and died in 1987. He was a poet and a scholar and an important voice in the resistance to the Soviet occupation. He was considered to be the "ablest living poet in the traditional Persian style."

*Aabdullah Ansari* was a poet from eleventh-century Herat. He died in 1089 and was best known for his *Munajat* or "Intimate Psalms."

*Saib-e-Tabrizi* was a seventeenth-century Persian poet.

*Nizami Ganjevi* was a twelfth-century Azerbaijanian poet. He wrote in Persian.

*Jalal ad-Din Rumi* was a thirteenth-century Sufi poet from Balkh. He is said to have created the whirling dance of the Mevlevi dervishes. This dance symbolizes the search for the Lost Beloved.

*Umar Khayyam (Omar Khayyam)* is known to western hemisphere readers through Edward Fitzgerald's translation of his *Rubaiyat*. The *Rubai* is a poetic form notable for having a consistent meter and four-line rhyming stanzas. His probable death date is 1132.

*Nur ad-Din Abd ar-Rahman Jami* was born in Kharjird in 1414 and died in Herat in 1492. He was a Sufi poet and was one of the great poets of his day.

Afghanistan, to readers in his new home. He writes in English, but sprinkles both works with Farsi or the Afghan variant of that language, Dari. *The Kite Runner*, including as it does the story of immigration and adjusting to a new country, would be the more likely candidate of Hosseini's two novels to be considered a novel of immigration or an ethnic novel; however, these issues are secondary to the main plot line of Amir's betrayal of his childhood friend and his quest to redeem himself. Amir and his father remain part of a cohesive Afghan community and within that community they share mutual respect and receive and provide protection and care as it is needed. Hosseini works into the story the struggles of the community in exile: the need to cope with a new language, the loss of status and material wealth, and the conflict of old ways amidst a population with vastly different values and customs. Rather than the comfortable homes and extravagant parties (e.g., Amir's birthday party) of their lives in Afghanistan, members of the community meet and socialize at the flea market—the great leveler of the community in exile. Hosseini depicts the way that the younger generation adapts more quickly to the language and customs of the new country. Although these young Afghan Americans do not lose their connection to the Afghan community and its beliefs and customs, they are able to move beyond that community and accept their new country.

## HOSSEINI WRITES LOVE STORIES

Finally, Hosseini, the storyteller, told an audience at the Central Parkway Library of the Free Public Library in Philadelphia, that both stories are first and foremost love stories.

> Both are love stories, they are both stories of love found in the most unlikely places. In *The Kite Runner* it was these two boys who came from different ends . . . polar ends of society and yet they were like brothers. In [*A Thousand Splendid Suns*] it is the story of this unlikely love between these two very, very different women . . . somehow they find each other and there is this very special bond between them. The connection between these two novels is this unlikely and improbable and human connection that redeems these characters.

He further described these novels when responding to a question about the "overriding message" of the novels:

> I don't think that *The Kite Runner* has appeal to people because it happens to be set in a country where there are American GI's. I think the reason people respond to that novel is because it is about very human things . . . that novel is about forgiveness and love, and friendship and loss and [*A Thousand*

*Splendid Suns*] is about love and it is first and foremost a love story. And those are [universal] human experiences. And so I hope that people walk away with the sense that [Afghanistan] is a remote country, it is an impoverished country; [Afghans] have a different culture, they have a different faith, but at the end of the day, people are people, they want the same things. They want their children to be safe, they want a roof over their heads, they want to be able to feed their families . . . when they are sick they want to see a doctor, and they want an education . . . and people are not very different from each other when it comes right down to it. (Transcribed from the Free Library of Philadelphia podcast, Hosseini 2007)

Hosseini's analysis of his work is straightforward. He looks to the tradition of storytelling and describes his novels as love stories, albeit uncommon love stories, with the universal theme of the power of love to bring redemption.

The form of the novel is fluid. It evolved out of the unique human desire to tell and to hear stories—the old image of people sitting around a fire telling stories that explained who we were and where we came from. Stories once were predominantly tales of god-like heroes and gods. The novel emerged as an art form for the everyday, the antihero, the accidental hero, the man down the street, or the woman on the bus. Hosseini may be a storyteller and his stories may be at heart love stories, but they are squarely stories written within the Western novel tradition. Our understanding of Hosseini's novels is enriched when we consider them within the literary tradition of novels of personal transformation; historical novels providing illumination to readers about country, time, and place; domestic novels providing insight into intimate family relationships taking place primarily within the four walls of the home; or ethnic and immigrant novels exploring the struggle of becoming part of the fabric of a new country.

The Ghazal comes directly out of the Persian literary tradition and is usually a poem of spiritual or personal love. (See Reuben Levy, *An Introduction to Persian Literature*, and Walid Ahmadi, *Modern Persian Literature in Afghanistan*.)

## DISCUSSION QUESTIONS

- Which type of novel described above do you feel best fits either *The Kite Runner* or *A Thousand Splendid Suns*? Talk about specific elements of the novel that lead you to make your choice.
- Thinking about what Michael Roemer, John Harrell, and Rosemary Horowitz have to say about oral tradition, can you see Hosseini's works within or at least emanating from that tradition? Talk about why and use examples from the novels.
- In what ways are Hassan, Laila, Mariam, and/or Amir transformed as the novels in which they figure progress? Do these characters display heroic characteristics? Explain your point of view.
- Talk about the quests of each character, how is the path of their life determined by their station within the social hierarchy? What were some of the life-changing decisions they made, and were they for good or ill?

# 3

# THE KITE RUNNER
# (2003)

*The Kite Runner* is Hosseini's first published novel. There are many ways to describe this novel, but Hosseini calls it a love story. It is not a conventional love story, however. It is the story of love between two friends who are also servant and master; the sins of commission and omission that tear the friendship apart; and the loyalty and altruistic love that survives in spite of everything. It is also the story of the love between father and son, husband and wife, and parent and child. The novel takes place across generations and continents, offers adventure, and provides a fresh look at the country and culture of Afghanistan. Page numbers cited for *The Kite Runner* are from the 2004 paperback edition (New York: Riverhead Books).

## *The Kite Runner*: A Plot Summary

Hosseini's *The Kite Runner* is divided into three major sections. The first part of the story takes place in Kabul. Amir, the main character and narrator of the novel, describes his childhood in the early to mid-1970s and, especially, his relationship with Hassan. This section includes the pivotal event of the narration. The second section begins in 1981 after Amir and his father leave Afghanistan during the Soviet occupation. This part of the novel takes place in Fremont, California, a city south of

San Francisco in the East Bay. Here, they live as part of an immigrant Afghan community in the Bay Area. This section ends with the marriage of Amir to Soraya and the death of Amir's father in 1989. In the final section of the novel, it is 2001 and Amir returns to Afghanistan by way of Pakistan. Amir receives a phone call from his mentor and his father's best friend, Rahim Khan, who asks Amir to visit. He tells Amir that he is sick, and that he has something for Amir to do that will help Amir "to be good again."

It is with the remembrance of this phone call that the novel opens. Rahim Khan's suggestion that Amir may have the opportunity to "be good again" brings the pivotal moment of Amir's childhood vividly to his mind and he takes the call as a sign that his past is catching up with him. Amir then begins to tell the story of his childhood and the reader is introduced to the main characters of the novel. Hassan is the servant to Amir, but also his childhood companion. Ali is Hassan's father, and, just as Amir has grown up with Hassan, Amir's father, Baba, grew up "as brothers" with Ali. Hassan and Ali live in a mud hut on the property of Baba and Amir.

Baba is a successful businessman and a powerful man in the community. He is known for helping those who are in need. His closest friend and associate, Rahim Khan is a gentle man and more sympathetic to Amir's quiet ways than Baba. Hassan and his father both suffer from physical deficiencies. Ali's face is paralyzed, making it difficult for him to show any expression, and Hassan was born with a cleft lip. According to Amir, Hassan's beautiful mother, Sanaubar, abandoned Hassan shortly after his birth due to this condition. Although Hassan and Ali have grown up as "brothers" or "friends" to Baba and Amir, it is clear that their positions are those of servant and master. Amir and his father are Sunni Muslim Pashtuns and Hassan and his father are Shi'a Hazara. The Hazara are a minority in Afghanistan and the Pashtun are the ruling majority. This is an important aspect of the novel, because of the inflexibility of the social division between Baba and Ali and Amir and Hassan. Because of the nature of the culture within Kabul and Afghanistan, they are divided by economic status, religion, and ethnicity.

Amir spends a good deal of time on his own or with Hassan. Neglected by his father, Amir feels responsible for the death of his mother who died in childbirth. He believes that his father has never forgiven him for this. While Baba is described as a physically imposing man, a bear wrestler in fact, as well as an important man in his community and nation, Amir is quiet and seemingly lacking in courage and determination. Hassan is intelligent, courageous, honest, and athletic. Amir notes that his father tends to favor Hassan. His desire for his

The Pashtuns are the ethnic majority in Afghanistan, and with the exception of the Soviet occupation and the present post–U.S. invasion era, it has been the Pashtuns that have ruled the country. Other major ethnic groups include the Tajiks, Hazaras, and Uzbeks. The population of Afghanistan, according to the Central Intelligence Agency's *World Factbook*, is divided as follows: 42 percent Pashtun, 27 percent Tajik, 9 percent Hazara, and 9 percent Uzbek. The remaining 13 percent of the population are Aimaks, Turkmen, Baloch, Nuristanis, Qirghiz, Farsiwan, Qizilbash, Hindus, and Sikhs.

father's attention and approval is powerful. Amir admits that he is jealous of his father's regard and affection for Hassan and he is not above lying to spend time on his own with his father or to place himself in a better light than Hassan. Amir overhears Baba telling Rahim Khan that he finds it hard to believe that Amir is his son and that he fears that Amir is missing an important character trait. "A boy who won't stand up for himself becomes a man who can't stand up to anything" (22). Rahim Khan is supportive of Amir. He suggests that Amir only lacks a mean streak, but later, Amir, who takes his father's perception of his shortcomings to heart, takes his hurt feelings out on Hassan and notes to himself that Rahim Khan was wrong about "the mean streak thing" (23).

As the story progresses, the reader learns more about Hassan's role in Amir's life. He works with Ali as a servant to the household. Each morning he prepares Amir's breakfast, irons his clothes, and gets his books and things ready for school. Hassan is illiterate as is his father. When Amir leaves for school in the car with his father, Hassan walks into town with his father to run errands for the household. Amir and Hassan often read together, but Amir has been careful to keep Hassan from learning to read. Always jealous of Hassan's physical superiority, he also worries that Hassan is smarter than him. He not only refuses to teach Hassan to read, but also makes fun of Hassan for not knowing certain things. Amir's position as "master" empowers him to treat Hassan with very little respect and Hassan's position as servant leads him to accept this treatment without overt comment or reaction. It is through these reading sessions, however, that Amir begins to dream up his own stories. After discovering that Hassan likes one of his stories, Amir returns home to write it up. Although his father shows little interest, Rahim Khan reads the story and praises Amir.

While Amir navigates his relationship with Hassan and with his father, large events are happening in Afghanistan. Former Prime Minister

Daoud overthrows King Zahir Shah, his cousin, in a bloodless coup, and then changes Afghanistan from a constitutional monarchy to a republic. Amir and Hassan experience a run-in with the psychotic bully Assef, who represents the worst of Afghanistan. Blonde and blue-eyed from his German mother, he professes admiration for Hitler and expresses his desire to treat the Hazara as Hitler treated the Jews, with the goal of preserving Afghanistan for the Pashtun. During this confrontation, Hassan defends Amir and himself from Assef with his slingshot. Assef backs down but promises to repay both Amir and Hassan, foreshadowing the novel's main crisis.

Time passes and, in the winter of 1974, Baba provides Hassan with plastic surgery to repair his cleft lip as a surprise birthday present. Amir is filled with jealousy once again, going so far as to envy Hassan's cleft lip wishing that he too could enjoy Baba's compassion. Filled with insecurity and resentment, Amir continues to challenge Hassan, testing his loyalty. When Hassan says that he would rather eat dirt than lie to Amir, Amir asks him if he really would. As they look at each other, Hassan breaks away briefly from his role as servant to ask Amir if he would really ask him to do this.

Despite these tensions, the two boys eagerly await the coming winter kite tournament. Amir's father buys them kites and they prepare their strings, or *tar,* with the requisite glass for cutting the *tar* of competing kites. Hosseini provides information about the Afghan tradition of kite flying and kite running. Hassan is a champion kite runner. It is especially praiseworthy to capture the last kite cut down in a tournament. So, not only do Hassan and Amir hope to outlast all the other kite flyers, they also hope to run down the final kite. At the kite competition, Hassan assists Amir by controlling the *tar.* When it becomes clear that the two will cut down the last kite, Amir genuinely embraces Hassan, letting all his feelings of jealousy drop away. Hassan is momentarily an equal in their victory, but then remembers that he must run the kite for Amir. He calls out to Amir as he runs off, "For you a thousand times over" (67). Amir stays behind and contemplates the triumph of presenting this last kite to his father. He feels acutely that his father blames him for the death of his mother, and he pins all his hope on this one moment of glory to reverse the years of exile from his father's love.

Later, he sets out to find Hassan. As he asks different people if they have seen him, they respond with derogatory comments about Hazaras and question Amir's concern for a mere servant and a Hazara servant at that. "Your Hazara?" and "What is a boy like you doing here at this time of the day looking for a Hazara. . . . What is he to you?" (68, 69). Amir never contradicts these abusive comments. When he finally finds

The traditional Afghan sport of kite fighting or *gudiparan bazi* was banned along with other activities and forms of celebration under the Taliban. Usually there is a kite flyer and someone who holds the drum with the wire and who advises the flyer on when to let out more wire. This wire is often coated with ground glass. The fight takes place when two kites come into contact. The victor in the fight cuts the wire of the opponent. A runner will then chase after the severed kite. The retrieved kite is kept as a trophy. (See David Sahar, "The Art of Gudiparan Bazi"; David Korzon, "A Storyteller's Story"; and "Afghan Kite History" at planet.kite.matrix.)

Hassan, he sees that Assef and his friends are confronting him. Amir struggles briefly with the desire to interfere, but he also sees the kite waiting behind Hassan. Assef is demanding the kite, and Hassan is "eating dirt" rather than giving the kite to Assef. Amir stays long enough to see Assef rape Hassan, and then he runs off both fearful for his own safety and unwilling to risk the loss of his kite. Amir waits a safe amount of time before going back to find Hassan. Hassan is clearly in pain, but Amir does not ask him about it and Hassan says nothing. Hassan gives the kite to Amir who takes it to Baba.

The friendship of Amir and Hassan deteriorates in the aftermath of the kite tournament and Assef's brutal attack on Hassan. Amir feels excruciating guilt but says nothing to Hassan. Rather than comfort him or in any way help him, Amir becomes distant and harshly unkind. Though he has gained some attention from his father as a result of his kite tournament triumph, he finds that he is unable to enjoy it. Amir says, "Everywhere I turned I saw signs of [Hassan's] loyalty, his goddamn unwavering loyalty" (89). Amir tries to provoke Hassan into getting angry or fighting with him, but Hassan, a loyal servant and friend, will never accept Amir's bate. Amir's anger is reminiscent of Assef's attack on Hassan. He is able to take advantage of Hassan because of his lower social status. He is in a position to humiliate Hassan and Hassan is not in a position to retaliate. In effect, Amir is now asking Hassan "to eat dirt" on a daily basis. At the gala birthday party thrown for him by his father, Amir watches Hassan wait on Assef and his family. He later talks privately with Rahim Khan who tells him about his youthful love for a young Hazara woman. Rahim Khan was not allowed to marry her because of her servant status. He tells Amir, "you don't order someone to polish your shoes one day and call them sister the next" (99). Later, Amir sets up Hassan by making it look as though he has stolen Amir's birthday watch and money. Hassan takes the blame, but he and his father decide to leave Baba and Amir's household. Baba is devastated, but as Ali points out to him, they no longer work for him, and he cannot stop them. They leave for Hazarajat, the homeland of the Hazaras.

This first section of the novel ends as Amir and his father escape the Soviet invasion of Afghanistan. They go first to Pakistan before immigrating to Fremont. They have left everything but a few personal items behind. Even as they escape, Baba demonstrates his courage and heroism, while Amir suffers from motion sickness and fear.

As the second section of *The Kite Runner* begins, Amir and his father are living in Fremont, California, part of an Afghan immigrant committee. The transition has been a welcome one for Amir. He is able to leave his past behind, but Baba mourns the loss of his past and he now works at a gas station. Amir graduates from high school at the age of twenty and chooses to go to community college to study creative writing. This does not please Baba, but he accepts it. Baba and Amir supplement their income and their social life by visiting garage sales and selling their merchandise at the Sunday flea market. The Afghan community has its own section, creating a small community. Afghan music plays, food and tea and gossip are shared. Amir explains that "mechanics and tailors" sell used goods "alongside of former ambassadors, out-of-work surgeons, and university professors" (138). It is at the flea market that Amir first meets General Taheri and his beautiful daughter Soraya. Amir is aware that there is some gossip associated with Soraya, but he is more intrigued by her beauty.

Amir falls in love with Soraya, his flea market princess. He finds excuses to stop by her family stall until the general, her father, chastises him. The reader learns about the fragility of a woman's honor, the delicate nature of courtship, and the effects of the Afghan community's penchant for gossip. At about this same time, Baba becomes sick and is diagnosed with lung cancer. He refuses treatment. When it becomes clear that Baba has little time left to live, Amir asks his father to go *khastegari* for him and to ask the general for the hand of his daughter Soraya. Baba makes the ritual visit and his request is granted. Soraya has a secret to reveal to Amir first before the engagement is settled. Amir wishes that he could tell his own secret, but does not.

---

The official visit made by the suitor or a representative of the suitor to the prospective bride's family is called *khastegari*. In *The Kite Runner*, Baba visits Soraya's family to present Amir's suit to the mother and father.

Amir and Soraya are married skipping the traditional engagement period because Baba does not have long to live. After the wedding, Amir and Soraya live with Baba. Soraya helps care for Baba and reads to him from Amir's stories. After Baba dies, Amir and Soraya move to their own house. Amir notes that he never attends a flea market again, signifying his separation from the womb of the Afghan community and his identification with his new country. Amir attends San Jose State and Soraya joins him there to earn her teaching certificate. The general wishes she would choose a career with more prestige. He even imagines her taking part, as he hopes for himself, in a new Afghan government. Amir publishes his first novel in 1989. The details of Amir's life, whether joyful and sorrowful are, once again, as in his youth, dwarfed by events in Afghanistan. Amir and Soraya celebrate his first novel as they struggle to have a child. They reject the option to adopt and Soraya's father proclaims adoption as being unsuitable for Afghans. Amir secretly believes that his inability to have a child is punishment for his sins against Hassan. At this same time, the Soviets are pulling out of Afghanistan, the Soviet system is crumbling, and Afghanistan falls into a destructive civil war.

The third section of the novel begins in June 2001 after Amir receives the phone call from Rahim Khan. Amir and Soraya are living in San Francisco. They have been married for fifteen years and are still childless. Amir has published several novels, and Soraya works as a teacher. Amir decides that he must go to Rahim Khan who is now in Pakistan.

Rahim Khan lives in a section of Peshawar known as Afghan Town due to the concentration of refugees from Afghanistan living there. He talks to Amir about the devastation caused by the Soviet occupation and then the civil war that raged in Kabul following the Soviet withdrawal. He describes the happiness everyone felt when the Taliban drove out the Northern Alliance. The rejoicing was short lived, however, as the Taliban policies and practices turned out to be draconian. Rahim Khan then begins to tell Amir about Hassan, who, with his wife, moved from Hazarajat to Kabul to help Rahim Khan with Amir and Baba's house. Their son is born there. There are many good parts to Rahim Khan's story of Hassan. Hassan tells some of his own story in three letters that he has written to Amir and given to Rahim Khan to deliver. Hassan has learned to read and write.

The story of Hassan has a tragic ending. Hassan and his wife stay on at the house after Rahim Khan leaves for Peshawar. They are murdered by the Taliban, who take over the house and send their son Sohrab to an orphanage. Rahim Khan tells Amir that one of the reasons he has asked him to come to Pakistan is that he wants Amir to go to Kabul to find Sohrab. Amir says that he cannot possibly go; he cannot risk everything he has to do this. Of course, this is exactly what Hassan has done for Amir even in his final act. Rahim Khan is angry with Amir knowing full well all that Hassan has done and suffered for Amir and his family. It is at this point that he tells Amir that Hassan is Baba's son. Amir is furious with his father for this deception and blames Rahim Khan for not telling him sooner.

After thinking everything over, Amir realizes that his actions have had a grave effect on Hassan's life. He now thinks of Hassan as his brother and he recalls the unqualified love Hassan has given him. Amir thinks about his father's desire for him to stand up for something and to do his own fighting and realizes that this is the time to do it. He returns to Rahim Khan's house and tells him that he is going to go to Kabul to find Sohrab.

Rahim Khan hires Farid to drive Amir to Kabul. Farid questions the sincerity of Amir's motives in returning to Afghanistan and suggests that Amir has always been a tourist in Afghanistan. They spend the night at the house of Wahid, who is Farid's brother. Amir tells Wahid about his search for Sohrab. This softens Farid, who tells Amir that he will help Amir find Sohrab. Farid and Amir drive to the orphanage in Karteh-Seh, a district within Kabul. The orphanage director, Zaman, is reluctant to let them in, but Amir explains that he is Sohrab's uncle and that he hopes to take Sohrab out of Afghanistan to care for him. The director lets them in and explains the meager resources he has to offer the children at the orphanage and the hardships they endure. He tells Amir and Farid that Sohrab has been taken from the orphanage by a Talib official; that, in fact, this official comes to the orphanage regularly to buy children. Farid goes into a murderous rage and tries to strangle the director. Amir stops Farid from killing the director and gives Zaman the chance to explain the impossible situation he is in. He receives no pay; he has sold everything he owns to support the orphanage; if he does not accept the money for one child the official will "take ten" (257). Zaman uses the money from the official to buy food for the children. Amir and Farid leave Zaman, with his glasses broken and the children clinging to him.

Zaman has instructed Amir and Farid on how to make contact with the Talib official. They are to go to a soccer game at Ghazi Stadium in Kabul. They sit through the first half of a soccer game, the Afghan players wearing long pants, the Talib guards keeping the crowds from making too much noise. During halftime, a cleric presides over a public execution. The Talib official, appearing as described by Zaman, throws the first stone. Following this bloody and murderous interlude, the game resumes. Farid and Amir are able to connect with the entourage of the official and arrange an appointment.

Amir's mother dies in childbirth. The infant mortality rates in Afghanistan for 1970, 1980, 2005, and 2008 are as follows:
  1970 *Total:* 215 per 1,000 live births
  1980 *Total:* 185 per 1,000 live births
  2005 *Total:* 165 per 1,000 live births
  2008 *Total:* 154.67 per 1,000 live births
  *From United Nations Statistics Division, "Key Global Indicators, Infant Mortality, Afghanistan 1960–2005", and Central Intelligence Agency, 2008 World Factbook.*

Amir makes the visit to the Talib official realizing this may be the last thing he does. He is not long into his interview before it becomes clear that the official knows Amir and it finally dawns on Amir that this is Assef. Hosseini portrays Assef unsparingly as a sadistic, psychopathic killer. Not only is he evil, but, as a Talib, his only principle seems to be one of eliminating the Hazara population. Assef taunts Amir, playing to Amir's fears. He brings out Sohrab who is dressed and decorated as a dancer. He has the boy dance and continues to provoke Amir by handling Sohrab in a clearly sexual manner. Amir becomes emboldened by his disgust and horror for Assef, who has described his part in the massacre at Mazar-i-Sharif, and his belief that Afghanistan should be left to the Pashtuns. Hosseini points to many contradictions and hypocrisies, drawing comparisons to Hitler and other genocidal leaders and regimes. The treatment of Sohrab by Assef mirrors Assef's treatment of Hassan and, to an extreme degree, Amir's attempt to disgrace and humiliate Hassan. The boy and his father are in a social class that expects to be and can be exploited and degraded. Their society condones it. Finally, Assef tells Amir that he can take the boy, but they will fight to the death over him. As Amir's teeth and bones are shattering, Amir feels the relief he has been looking for all these years. He is finally experiencing atonement. But, Sohrab is screaming in the background and he begs Assef to stop beating Amir. He threatens Assef with his slingshot as his father did nearly three decades earlier. This time, however, he follows through with the threat and he shoots a metal ball into Assef's eye. Sohrab, just a child, calls to Amir to leave with him; he helps him up and together they leave the building. Assef is screaming in pain in the background, the ball lodged in his eye socket. Farid is there to help Sohrab and Amir into the car and they drive away as Amir drifts into unconsciousness.

Farid has taken Sohrab and Amir back to Peshawar. Amir is in and out of consciousness as he is treated for his injuries, which include seven broken ribs, a ruptured spleen, a broken eye socket bone, broken teeth, a punctured lung, and, most symbolically, a mouth split in two. His injuries have been addressed, his mouth has been sewn up. A small scar, not unlike that of Hassan's repaired cleft lip, will be all that remains of that injury. It is now time to care for Sohrab and make arrangements for his well-being.

Events and circumstances determine that Amir should take Sohrab with him to the United States, but it is not easy. Amir first promised Sohrab that he would not leave him in an orphanage, but he goes back on this promise thinking that he may need to leave Sohrab in Pakistan temporarily. This uncertainty leads Sohrab to attempt suicide. Amir discovers Sohrab just after hearing from Soraya that she has made arrangements to bring Sohrab into the country through her family connections. Amir reconnects with his Muslim heritage as he promises devotion to God in return for Sohrab's life. Sohrab does recover physically, but his emotional mending takes much longer. He returns to the United States with Amir but accompanies him out of resignation rather than desire. Many months go by and Sohrab remains silent. He goes through the motions of his day without any engagement with others. *The Kite Runner* does not end with everything resolved, but Amir reports a tiny miracle. At a gathering in the park for the Afghan New Year, Soraya notices that Sohrab has taken an interest in the kite-flying contests. Amir buys a kite and tries to persuade Sohrab to fly it with him. Although Sohrab does not participate, he does follow Amir. After he successfully cuts a competitor's kite, Amir offers to run the kite for Sohrab, telling him, "For you, a thousand times over" (371), recalling Hassan's promise to Amir at the fateful kite competition so many years ago. The novel ends on a note of hope that Sohrab will recover and become a full part of Amir and Soraya's family.

## LOSING AND RECLAIMING AFGHANISTAN: THE SETTING OF *THE KITE RUNNER*

*The Kite Runner* begins and ends in San Francisco. As the novel opens, Amir is working as a writer, living with his wife in San Francisco. He is an American citizen, educated in American schools and universities, writing his novels in English. His boyhood in Afghanistan seems to be very far behind him until he receives the fateful phone call from Rahim Khan, a voice he has not heard since leaving his homeland. This phone call leads Amir to recall his boyhood in Kabul and the life-changing event that inevitably leads to this particular phone call. In this portion of the novel, Amir describes a Kabul lined with trees, a Kabul where a child can roam the streets and fields without fear of land mines, where the appealing aroma of food fills the air, where kites are flown, and where movies are attended. Although he was not a particularly happy child, he had a life of material comforts.

Hosseini frames his book with these locations as Amir leaves San Francisco for Afghanistan and then finally returns to San Francisco to end the novel. It is in the third section of the novel that Amir returns to Afghanistan by way of Pakistan. In his phone call, Rahim Khan has asked Amir to come to see him and offers him the "chance to be good again." Amir first goes to Peshawar, the destination for many Afghan refugees, to visit Rahim Khan in what the taxi-driver calls Afghan Town. "Many of your brothers in this area, *yar*. They are opening businesses, but most of them are very poor" (196). From there, Amir sets out for his return trip to Afghanistan and Kabul to look for Hassan's son, Sohrab. The Kabul of his return visit is nothing like the Kabul he grew up in. The Soviet occupation left Kabul mostly untouched, but the civil war following the departure of the Soviets has left Kabul in ruins and its population crippled and in extreme poverty. Additionally, the street presence of the Taliban means that it can be dangerous to move around openly in the streets. Amir revisits his home, visits an orphanage, and attends a public event at Ghazi Stadium. Amir sums up Kabul in three words, "Rubble and Beggars" (245).

Following his rescue of Sohrab, Amir returns with him to Peshawar and then they go to Islamabad before returning together to San Francisco where the novel ends. Amir is returning to an established life, family, and routine, but Sohrab will be beginning the long process of adjustment and recovery from yet another traumatic episode in his life. It is another generation that is escaping from the disaster of war in Afghanistan. Sohrab has much more to overcome than did Amir upon his arrival in the United States, but there is hope that the stability and love that Amir and Soraya will provide eventually will give Sohrab what he needs to thrive. The hope for this transformation arises out of a kite-flying activity that is part of the celebration of the Afghan New Year. So, although Sohrab is in a country that is drastically unlike anything he has experienced in his short life, he finds familiar vestiges of his culture and its celebrations, languages, and food just as Amir and his father found comfort in the Afghan community in Fremont.

In between the framing first and third sections to *The Kite Runner*, Amir and his father are living in Fremont, California, in the East Bay of the San Francisco Bay Area, and home to one of the largest Afghan communities in the United States. In this intermediate stage, Amir and his father adjust to life in a new country, in a vastly different culture, and under reduced circumstances both in terms of their economic and social status. Their transition is cushioned, however, by the closely knit community of Afghans, many of whom knew or knew of each other before coming to the United States, and who share the same customs, religion, perspectives, language, and food. They also share the pain of exile and the longing for homeland. The Afghan section of the flea market is an interesting and colorful symbol of the changes that the immigrants have endured: the leveling off of social hierarchy and the loss of livelihood, as well as the importance and desire to maintain as much of a way of life as is possible in an alien country.

In this transition segment, Amir loses his father and distances himself to a certain extent from the Afghan immigrant community. He has been shaped by the American education system and has chosen the unlikely career of writer. He has married an Afghan woman, but she has, in the same way as Amir, been influenced and shaped by her family's adopted country. After his marriage and the death of his father, Amir gives up the flea market and he and his wife move to San Francisco, removing themselves from the midst of the community that has watched over them, but not leaving it behind entirely.

## MAKING CHOICES: THE CHARACTERS OF *THE KITE RUNNER*

### Amir and Hassan, Baba and Ali

The central characters of *The Kite Runner* are Amir and Hassan and Baba and Ali. Amir is the main character and narrator of *The Kite Runner*. The reader sees everything from his perspective. As he looks back at his story, he has no kind words for himself. The strengths that Amir did have as a child, especially his knowledge of and ability to memorize the classic poetry of Afghanistan, are not appreciated by his father. Amir has not forgiven himself for his childhood betrayal of his servant and friend, Hassan, and so his view of his past is told through a lens of guilt and remorse. Conversely, Amir portrays Hassan as a saint. He not only is smart and athletic, but also is a loving, selfless, loyal, and patient friend. Hassan later returns to Kabul at Rahim Khan's request to help care for Baba and Amir's house, and in the end, he sacrifices his life in his attempt to protect the house from marauders. The fact of Hassan's servitude colors both Amir's attitude toward Hassan and Hassan's toward Amir. In addition, Amir is from the dominant ethnic group and religious sect. He is Pashtun and Sunni. Hassan is Hazara and Shi'a, the ethnic group most discriminated against in Afghanistan and the minority

King Mohammed Nadir Shah ruled Afghanistan from 1929 until his assassination in 1933. Amir's grandfather's picture dates from 1931. It is at once a symbol of Amir's family's station in the Afghanistan social hierarchy and a symbol of the elusive nature of positions of power within that same hierarchy.

religious sect. When the bully Assef first expresses disgust toward Hassan because of his Hazaran ethnicity and then asks Amir how he can call Hassan his friend, Amir recalls nearly saying, *"But he's not my friend! . . . He's my servant!"* (41). Amir goes on to wonder why, if Hassan is truly his friend, he only plays with him when no one else is around. As if these barriers were not significant enough, Amir is also deeply jealous of Hassan because of the affection and attention Baba shows to him.

Baba is Amir's father and Ali is Hassan's father. Baba is a wealthy and influential man. Well connected, he is used to speaking his mind and having his way. Baba is noted for fighting bears and Amir likens him to a bear. His physicality and outgoing nature are a clear contrast to the insecure and bookish Amir. Baba is worldly. He has traveled to other countries and has an extensive library of which Amir makes heavy use. Ali is the lifelong servant of Baba. As such, he is unassuming and quiet. He is an object of ridicule for many of the children in the district who mock his Hazaran features and the paralysis that affects his face and legs. But, like Hassan who perhaps learned this trait from him, Ali is patient and does not respond to his tormentors.

Baba and Ali share a relationship similar to that of Amir and Hassan. Baba likes to talk about how he grew up playing daily with Ali as though they were brothers, and yet, Ali is clearly Baba's servant. He lives in a mud hut in the yard and serves the needs of the household as did his parents and as does his son. He was raised to serve and Baba to lead. Despite this inequitable situation, Hassan's childhood is possibly happier and more stable than Amir's. Despite the traumatic events that play out and Amir's betrayal, Hassan has the love and support of his father. When it becomes clear that it is an untenable situation for Hassan to continue to live near and to serve Amir, his father places loyalty to Baba's household second to his loyalty to his son. This causes Baba both shame and sorrow. When Rahim Khan describes Hassan's life after leaving Kabul for Hazarajat with his father, it is clear that he grew and prospered once out from under the limitations of his position of servitude.

## Rahim Khan, Friend of the Family

Although Amir's father did not appreciate Amir's interest in books and writing, Amir received encouragement and support from his father's closest friend, Rahim Khan. Rahim stays behind in Kabul after Baba and Amir leave the country. He stays on at Baba's family estate to care for and protect it. Later, he searches for Hassan to ask him to return to Kabul to help him care for the property. Hassan refuses at first, acknowledging that he is happy with his life in Hazarajat. He has married Farzana who is expecting their first child. He later, fatefully, changes his mind and returns with his wife to live with Rahim in his old home in Kabul. Although Rahim begs Hassan and Farzana to live in the house with him, they choose to live in the mud hut. Farzana gives birth to Sohrab, and Hassan and his family live happily for a time until, after Rahim leaves for Pakistan because of his health, militiamen murder Hassan and Farzana as they defend Baba's house. Sohrab is sent to an orphanage in Kabul.

## The Mothers

Both Amir and Hassan lost their mothers at birth. Sanaubar is Hassan's mother. It is said that Ali married her, his first cousin, as a favor to his uncle. Ali's marriage to Sanaubar, beautiful and notoriously "unscrupulous" as a young woman, would be a way for his uncle to retain his honor. She runs off with a band of musicians and dancers a week after Hassan is born. As she despised her husband for his age and physical failings, she also expressed disgust with her newborn son. Later Sanaubar returns to the mud hut in Kabul and is forgiven and taken in by Hassan and Farzana. Sanaubar helps to care for their newborn child, Sohrab. As it turns out, Baba had a brief affair with Sanaubar, and Hassan is his biological son. If Ali knows this, he does not reveal that he does, nor does this knowledge lessen his devotion to his son. Amir's mother, Sophia Akrami, died in giving birth to him. This fact is one of the major barriers between Amir and his father. Although Baba does not say so, Amir is sure that his father blames him for the death of his mother, and he feels his own sense of responsibility for her death. Sophia Akrami was "a highly educated woman universally regarded as one of

> Hazarajat is the national homeland of the Hazaras within Afghanistan. It includes the provinces of Bamiyan, Daikundi, and Ghor. It is a mountainous region in the central part of Afghanistan.

In a May 25, 2003, article in the *New York Times*, Dr. Peter Salama, director of the United Nations Children's Fund (UNICEF) in Afghanistan, is quoted as saying that Afghanistan has the highest maternal mortality rate in the world, with as many as 2,000 maternal deaths per 100,000 live births. Afghanistan's infant mortality rate is the fourth highest in the world. The United Nations cites 1,800 maternal deaths per 100,000 births in 2005 but also states that the statistics are derived from a model. (See Carlotta Gall, "Afghan Motherhood in a Fight for Survival," and United Nations Statistics Division, Millennium Development Goals Database.)

Kabul's most respected, beautiful, and virtuous ladies" (15). She taught classic Farsi literature at the university and was a descendant of the royal family. Sophia is an idealized ghost that haunts both Baba and Amir.

## Three Bullies

Although Amir claims that he only plays with Hassan when no one else is around, he does not mention any other friends. He seems to spend much of his time alone. The only other young people mentioned by Amir are the three bullies Assef, Wali, and Kamal. Assef is the ringleader, the psychotic bully who instigates the rape of Hassan in the novel's pivotal scene. His hapless parents, father Mahmood, an airline pilot, and mother, Tanya, from Germany, appear to have no control over their Hitler-admiring son. Hosseini describes Assef as blonde, blue-eyed, and tall. His character might easily be seen as symbolic of the British and Russians who vied for Afghanistan in the nineteenth century in what historians call "The Great Game." In fact, Assef could symbolize any country, including the Soviet Union and the United States, that has sought to lay claim to Afghanistan. Assef embodies the religious and ethnic intolerance that Hosseini sees as the dark side of Afghan culture. Wali and Kamal are followers, but they cannot bring themselves to participate in Assef's brutality. Assef appears later in the third section of the novel as the ruthless and still psychotically violent leader of the Taliban who has taken Sohrab to be his child-slave.

## The Taheris

Amir's bride-to-be and her mother and father are central characters in the second section of *The Kite Runner*. Amir catches sight of Soraya at the flea market where he and his father have a booth for selling their garage sale finds. Amir is almost immediately smitten and nearly undermines his chances of formally courting her by not abiding by the strict social guidelines of the Afghan community. Within these guidelines, when Soraya tells Amir what she is reading after he has asked, she jeopardizes her good reputation. Soraya's parents watch her closely because she has already disgraced the family by running off with a young man, thus causing them to move from Virginia to Fremont. Her father, Mr. Iqbal Taheri was a decorated general in Kabul and he worked for the Ministry of Defense. Unlike Baba, who works at a gas station and refuses any kind of aid, General Taheri accepts government assistance rather than work at a job beneath his status. He expects to be able to return to serve his country as soon as the Mujahideen defeat the Russians and the monarchy is restored. His wife and Soraya's mother, Jamila, had been a well-known singer of folk songs, *ghazals*, and raga in Kabul, but the general does not allow her to sing in public, and this is, in fact, part of their marriage contract. Singing is for those with lesser reputations. When Amir begins to stop by the Taheri booth at the flea market, Jamila becomes hopeful that he may wish to marry Soraya.

## Those Who Stayed Behind

Several new characters are introduced in the final section of the novel. Rahim Khan arranges for an Afghan driver, Farid, to take Amir into Afghanistan. Farid clearly resents Amir. He sees him as one of the many who left Afghanistan during the hard times, only to return to profit from the misery they left behind. Amir sees some truth in Farid's description, although he is not returning to Afghanistan to profit from the chaos. Farid stops for the night at Wahid and Maryam's house. They are his brother and sister-in-law. That night, Amir experiences the typical Afghan hospitality, where the hosts serve the guests even though the family must go without food for them to do so. Amir tells Wahid about his search for Sohrab, and upon learning of this mission, Farid softens and offers to help Amir. Amir relies on Farid throughout his stay in Afghanistan.

Amir and Farid's search for Sohrab takes them to the orphanage in Karteh-Seh, where they meet the director, Zaman. Zaman informs them that Sohrab has been taken by a Talib leader, and not only that, this leader comes for children on a regular basis. Although Farid and Amir are appalled and disgusted with Zaman for allowing the children to be taken, it becomes clear that there is no obvious path for Zaman to take. Zaman illustrates the complexities and moral ambiguities that dire conditions create. Sometimes, there are only evil solutions. In this case, it is the fate of the one child weighed against the fate of all of the children. Hosseini makes this clear when he portrays Amir watching Zaman as he and Farid drive away. Zaman's glasses are broken from Farid's attack, but the children cling to him. He is all they have, and Zaman has sacrificed all that he has for them.

## AFGHANISTAN, FORGIVENESS, AND EXILE: THEMES IN *THE KITE RUNNER*

Hosseini accomplishes three things with his novel *The Kite Runner*: he introduces the English-speaking reader to Afghanistan, he looks at the universal theme of transgression and forgiveness, and he explores the concept of homeland and exile. In his portrait of Afghanistan, Hosseini focuses on Kabul during the decades leading up to the Soviet invasion and under the Taliban. Hosseini presents not only the beauty and culture of the Afghanistan of his childhood but looks at its societal failings, including its religious divisions and ethnic discrimination. The theme of transgression and forgiveness is threaded throughout the entire novel. Primarily, Amir seeks forgiveness and redemption for his treatment of his childhood friend and servant Hassan, but other central and tangential characters in the novel also seek forgiveness and redemption. Finally, Hosseini follows his characters into exile in a strange country, the not-so-glamorous city of Fremont, California. Most dramatically, Amir's powerful and influential father is reduced to working in a gas station. The elite members of Amir's father's social network find their community at the local flea market. And although Amir breaks away from this community in some respects, he and his wife Soraya rely on this intricate familial and social network.

This social network within Afghanistan, or more specifically Kabul, is apparent as Amir describes his father's prominent and influential position in government and with members of the community. The oft-mentioned photograph of Baba's father with King Nadir Shah provides evidence of their importance among the ruling elite of Afghanistan. Afghanistan is a small country and the ruling elite are centered in Kabul, creating a world of their own. Baba is known by all and has helped many in the community from all levels within the social structure of the city. Kabul is a bustling city and, through his characters, Hosseini describes abundance, beauty, and a socially vibrant environment. There are open markets, shops, and artisans; there are rich aromas; there is a sense of community and promise. Amir has everything and more than he wants materially. Hassan has nothing beyond his loving father and their mud hut and the castoffs from Amir, but he benefits from the affection and generosity of Baba. The boys attend the movies and grow up thinking that Clint Eastwood speaks Farsi. This is a rich world, one in which people prosper and there is much to enjoy in daily life. This might be a different picture from what average news-watching Americans have in mind when they think of Afghanistan.

Hosseini does not just present an idyllic Afghanistan. The crises presented by Hosseini in the novel stem from inherent weaknesses in Afghanistan's social structure and its cultural prejudices. Amir and his father are Pashtun and Sunni Muslims, and their servants are Hazara and Shi'a Muslims. This is a typical servant-master arrangement. Hazara were often illiterate because they lacked education opportunities. They were seen as ethnically and religiously inferior to the Sunni Pashtuns. Although Baba loves Hassan and Ali, they will always be servants. Ali and Baba and Amir and Hassan might be "like brothers," but a power dynamic makes it possible for Amir to treat Hassan as an inferior, and that allows him to humiliate Hassan without fearing retribution. This same power structure allows Assef to rape Hassan without fear of reprisal, and assures him that he is unlikely to be stopped by casual observers. It is starkly apparent later in the novel when Assef has become a Talib leader. Although Amir's treatment of Hassan is not physically violent in the way that Assef's is, it is spiritually damaging to Hassan. This Pashtun disdain for the Hazara carries over into the Afghan community's exile in Fremont, California. As a child, Amir reads history and learns about the ways the Hazara people have been treated by the ruling Pashtun majority. He hears the slurs and knows that they are wrong, but he has never contradicted them. As an adult, and as he learns that Hassan was not just "like his brother," but, indeed, was in all ways his brother, Amir is able to speak against expressed prejudice.

Amir has a greet need for redemption. His betrayal and rejection of Hassan haunt him as a child and throughout his adult years. He sees his and his wife's inability to have a child as his punishment for his history with Hassan. His antipathy to Hassan has roots in the neglect he feels from his father. Amir's mother died giving birth to him, and he carries

---

The two branches of the Muslim faith are Sunni and Shi'a. Most Pashtuns are Sunni and they make up the majority religion in Afghanistan. Most Hazaras are Shi'a, and are thus further discriminated against by the ruling classes for their different religious practices.

this guilt with him. When his father shows so much interest in and affection for Hassan, Amir feels this intensely. He is jealous and resentful. These feelings drive him to cruelty. But it is also his youth, inexperience, and lack of guidance that mar his judgment. As Rahim Khan reminds him when they meet up again in Pakistan, he was just a child when all of these things happened. Amir achieves his redemption by rescuing Sohrab from Assef and, perhaps, even more important to him, through the brutal beating he receives at Assef's hands.

But Amir is not the only person seeking forgiveness in this novel. The character Zaman, the director of the orphanage, is a striking example. Almost a saint, Zaman has sacrificed all that he has to keep the orphanage afloat during the years of the Taliban. The children have very little food, and many are there because their mothers are unable to provide them with food. But Zaman, when pressed, allows some of the children to be sold. He defends his actions by pointing out that if he were not to comply, all the children would suffer. He receives a small amount of money that he uses to feed the remaining children. Amir's guide, Farid, attacks Zaman physically, and Amir is disgusted with Zaman, but Zaman is in a complex situation, and there is no clear path to what is right. He can only choose from among bad choices. As Amir drives away, Zaman stands in front of the orphanage, his glasses smashed from Farid's blows and the children clinging to him. Sohrab must learn to forgive himself and Amir. Like Amir, Sohrab feels guilty for events beyond his control. Amir blames himself for his mother's death, and Sohrab blames himself for what Assef has forced him to do. Sohrab must also learn to forgive and trust Amir, who promises Sohrab that he will never go to an orphanage again, but within days, Amir retracts this promise. Sohrab's road to forgiveness and healing is long, but it is not impossible. Amir, as well as the other characters, must come to terms with their failings and find forgiveness from within. Hosseini does not ask the reader to feel sorry for his characters; he portrays them as proud and, for the most part, self-sufficient. But they treasure their relationships and prosper through ingenuity and mutual support. Eventually, Amir moves away from his Afghan community, but it is through these close ties, developed through family and social networks, that Amir and Soraya are able to expedite Sohrab's entrance into the United States.

These familial and social networks, often intertwined, are all that the members of the Afghan exiled community have left after leaving their homeland. They arrive on American shores with severely reduced means, reduced influence, a language barrier to overcome, and an inability to find work that meets their training and expertise. Surrounded by a culture quite different from their own, the parents begin to lose authority over their children as their children quickly adapt to their new surroundings. Amir's father finds work as a gas station attendant, and he and Amir sell items they scavenge from garage sales at flea markets. Amir graduates from high school at the age of twenty and goes on to attend community college. Soraya's father was a general and refuses to work beneath his station in the United States, holding out hope that he will be able to return to Afghanistan and resume his former responsibilities. As the children move away, customs become harder to maintain. Amir finds that when he returns to Afghanistan, he is barely welcome, and he is unfamiliar with the country he once considered home.

## DISCUSSION QUESTIONS

- In chapter 2, Hosseini sets the background of the novel, describing the main characters, the pertinent social history of Afghanistan, and the social context for the plot, including ethnic and religious divisions. He works these details into the narrative of the story. What are some of the techniques he uses to inform the reader of these details without abandoning the persona of the narrator?
- How does the fact that Amir is looking back on his childhood color his narrative? Do you trust the character's judgment and memory? For instance, Hassan is superior in every way to Amir. How would you interpret Amir's memory of this? Is it realistic and how does it contribute to the plot and themes of the novel?
- What do we learn about Hassan as a character in the very first chapter?
- What do we learn about Amir in that same chapter and how does his personality or character contrast with Hassan's?
- Talk about the significance of Hassan's illiteracy and the fact that after leaving Baba and Amir's compound he learns to read and write.
- How did you feel when Rahim Khan talks Hassan and his family into leaving their home to return to Kabul to take care of Baba's compound?
- Amir tells us that he and Hassan grew up together, were nursed by the same woman, and spent their days playing together. How do you react to the use of the term brother to describe their relationship?
- How does the fact that Amir is telling the story affect what we know about the different characters in the book?
- Think about Amir's influence on the representation of the details of the story as you read through the novel. Is he honest with the readers? Does he protect himself?

- If you think he is being honest with the readers, what would motivate him to present himself in such a compromised light?
- How are Ali and Baba different both physically and by personality? How are they different kinds of fathers? How have their personalities and paternal roles influenced their sons?
- Can you see the physical descriptions of Ali and Baba as metaphorical? If so, to what purpose?
- How do you react to Amir's feelings about Hassan?
- Hosseini sprinkles Dari words throughout the text. What effect does this have on the tone of the novel?
- What is your reaction to Assef? Is he a realistic character? In what way can his character be seen as a metaphor?
- How does the story of Hassan's plastic surgery move the plot of the novel along?
- When describing kite fighting and running, Amir says that "Afghans cherish customs but abhor rules" (52). Do the characters in *The Kite Runner* exhibit this characteristic? How do rules differ from customs?
- Have Hosseini's descriptions of Kabul and Afghanistan before the Soviet invasion changed how you think of the country? How would you describe the city and the country if all you knew about them was what you had read in this novel?
- Racism in Afghanistan is very much like racism in America. Where do you see the similarities? How do you see this racism in the relationship of Ali and Hassan to Baba and Amir's household? Is there any irony intended in the way Baba talks about Ali being "like a brother" or "like a son" to his own father? What are the differences between the way Baba professes to feel for Ali and Hassan and the way we interpret Amir's feelings?
- Do you blame Baba for not getting involved in the deterioration of Amir and Hassan's "friendship"? What might have been different if he had? Does Hosseini provide clues to Afghanistan's culture that would explain Baba's protective feelings toward Hassan but unwillingness to get involved or even to ask Ali about how Hassan is doing?
- Amir describes Soraya the first time he sees her (140). What do you learn from this description?
- Amir describes his and his father's junking expeditions and flea market activities. What do we learn from his description of these activities and the flea market? Hosseini gives the reader extensive information about Amir and his father's life in the United States as well as about Afghan refugees more generally. What do we learn about his description of this life?

- In the second half of the book, Amir's relationship with his father seems to have changed. What accounts for this?
- The Afghan community gravitates toward the flea market, and Baba does not want to give it up after he is diagnosed with cancer. What is it about the flea market that attracts Baba and the community?
- Amir and Soraya have spent enough time in the United States to have adopted American ways. In her past, Soraya ran off with an Afghan man who did not respect her honor. She has defied her family but come back to them. Despite their more American ways and outlooks, they are still governed by the ways of their parents who live by the more rigid Afghan codes. Soraya's future is at stake, but Amir has quite a bit of freedom. What are the good and bad aspects of maintaining a culture in a foreign country? What kind of upbringing would you expect the children of Soraya and Amir to have compared with their own upbringing?
- Farid says Amir has always been a tourist in Afghanistan, but when Amir is finally back in Afghanistan he says, "After all these years, I was home again, standing on the soil of my ancestors" (240). How do you interpret this, and would you agree with Farid or Amir? Support your opinion.
- Think about the difference in how Amir describes Kabul during his youth and what he sees upon his return. How does this serve the purposes of the novel? Do you think Amir's memories are accurate?
- Talk about the character of Zaman, the orphanage director. His situation is complex. Is he to be condemned or honored?
- As Farid and Amir become closer, Farid questions Amir's judgment in risking so much to rescue a Shi'a. Compare the elements of racism and cultural and religious discrimination latent in Afghanistan as described by Hosseini through Amir's story with those of the United States.

# 4

# A THOUSAND SPLENDID SUNS
# (2007)

In *A Thousand Splendid Suns* Hosseini returns to Afghanistan and once more offers his readers a love story. As in *The Kite Runner*, the relationships are complicated and diverse. There is first and foremost the love between two women, supporting each other in their marriage to the same man. There is also a more traditional love story—a childhood romance that at first seems hopeless and then becomes reality. All of this is set in the midst of war and famine over three decades in both the cities and countryside of Afghanistan. The two women are quite different from one another and were raised in completely different words, although within the same country. They nonetheless forge a strong bond of family and friendship. Page numbers cited for *A Thousand Splendid Suns* are from the 2007 hardcover edition (New York: Riverhead Books).

## *A Thousand Splendid Suns*: A Plot Summary

Mariam is five years old when the novel opens. She is waiting for her father Jalil to arrive for his weekly visit. Mariam is Jalil's illegitimate daughter. Her mother, Nana, was a servant in Jalil's household when she became pregnant. The family was outraged and Nana and Mariam were thrown out of the house. Nana's life is bitter. She has been discarded by Jalil and disowned by her father; Nana's mother died when she was two.

She resents Mariam's devotion to Jalil and is cynical about his kind-
nesses to her. Nana is very harsh with Mariam and tells her that she is
an unwanted thing, a *harami*. Jalil may come only once a week, but he is
kind and gentle and brings Mariam gifts. Nana warns Mariam not to have
faith in her father or men in general. She tells her, "Like a compass needle
that points north, a man's accusing finger always finds a woman" (7). This
sentence comes back to haunt Mariam throughout the novel.

Mariam and her mother live on the outskirts of her mother's village
of Gul Daman. They receive few visitors because Nana prefers to be left
on her own. One of their regular visitors is Mullah Faizullah. He teaches
Mariam to read and write, to read and recite the Koran, and to say her
prayers. He is attentive and good to her. Mariam asks him to ask her
mother if she can go to school. She has just heard that her father's other
daughters have begun school. When her mother hears about Mariam's
wish she responds harshly and tells Mariam that it is not her place to
attend school. Nana tells her that she has only one skill to learn, and
that is to endure (17).

Mariam's week is spent in anticipation of Jalil's arrival. She imagines
what it would be like to live in Herat with Jalil experiencing the excite-
ment of the big city, caring for Jalil and attending to his needs. When he
visits on her birthday, Jalil tells Mariam that she can ask for anything.
She asks him to take her to his cinema. They negotiate on this point for
some time until Jalil agrees to meet her the next day at noon. He does
not come, and Mariam decides to walk to Herat to find him. She does
this against her mother's will. When Mariam arrives, she is enchanted
with the bustle, the flowers and trees, the abundance on the streets.
Everything is fantastic and lovely. A kindly taxi driver takes her to Jalil
Khan's house. When she arrives, Mariam is not admitted in. She is told
that Jalil Khan is away. The family chauffeur urges her to go home and

---

Gul Daman is a small village just outside of Herat. Herat is one of the
largest cities in Afghanistan with an estimated population in 2006 of
349,000. Compare this to Kabul's 2006 population of 2,536,300.
Afghanistan's total estimated population according to a CIA 2008 esti-
mate is 32,738,376. The last official census was taken in 2006. Hosseini writes in his acknowledgments that the village of Gul Daman is
fictional. *Gul* means flower, *Daman* may be a term for the area spread-
ing out around the foot of the hills. (See Europa Publications Limited,
*South Asia: 2008*.)

offers to drive her, but she refuses and spends the night on the doorstep. In the morning, the chauffeur insists on taking her home and picks her up and puts her in the car, but not before Mariam catches a glimpse of Jalil Khan in the window. When she arrives back at her home, or *kolba*, Mariam discovers that her mother has committed suicide.

After the funeral, Jalil Khan takes Mariam back to his house. She is given a guestroom. Although she is not encouraged to come out of the room, she also chooses not to. She receives visits from Bibi jo, a family friend, and Mullah Faizullah. Their genuine care and kindness for her contrast starkly with Jalil's more cautious attention. Mullah Faizullah tries to comfort Mariam who is disconsolate. He tells Mariam that she need not feel responsible for her mother's death. At the end of the week, Mariam is told by one of Jalil's wives that she must go downstairs. Jalil and his wives are waiting for Mariam at the large imposing dining room table. At this meeting, she finds out that the wives have found her a suitor. His name is Rasheed and he is a Pashtun who lives in Kabul; he is forty-five and he is a shoemaker. Mariam is horrified, but when she begs her father to stop this from happening, the wives tell her that he has already given his consent. Mariam realizes that they not only want to marry her off to get her out of the house, but they also want her as far away as possible, because she is a symbol of shame to them. When Afsoon, one of the wives, walks Mariam back to her room, she also locks her in. Mariam has lost her freedom and has no say or power to determine the course that her life will take. Mariam will be engaged the next day, and she will leave on the bus for Kabul that same afternoon.

As forewarned, the *nikka* takes place the next day. The mullah rushes through the ceremony so that Rasheed and Mariam can make the bus to Kabul. Looking in the mirror, part of the traditional ceremony, Mariam sees her own face and the face of her husband for the first time. Mariam must answer for herself that she will accept Rasheed, and, although she hesitates, she does answer affirmatively. At the bus, Mariam lets Jalil know that she is finished with him and that she never wants to see him again.

The first year of Mariam's life with Rasheed passes with its difficulties and rewards. Rasheed has moments of kindness and regard, but is also possessive and ill tempered. He requires Mariam to wear a burqa. It is heavy, awkward, and stifling, but she feels protected and shielded by it. She sees it as a one-way window from which she can view the world, but through which the world cannot see or judge her. She finds Rasheed's desire to keep her away from other men as a sign of his regard and she feels both treasured and significant. During this first year she experiences her first restaurant, her first ice cream, sex with her husband, and she becomes pregnant. Mariam feels so much happiness when she realizes that she is pregnant. She immediately imagines the blessings of motherhood. Rasheed is also pleased, but also determined to have a boy. Sadly, Mariam has a miscarriage, and with this miscarriage goes her happiness and Rasheed's regard. After four years of marriage, Mariam learns that Rasheed's moods and tempers are to be feared. She has suffered six more miscarriages and, with each one, Rasheed becomes more distant and abusive. It is 1978, and Mariam is nineteen. The Communists take over the presidential palace in Kabul and massacre President Daoud and his family. Down the street from Mariam and Rasheed, a woman named Fariba has given birth to a new baby, a daughter who she and her husband name Laila.

In part two, the story jumps to 1987. Laila is nine years old and she has become fast friends with the boy next door, Tariq. Laila's mother spends much of her time in bed, brokenhearted over the absence of her sons who are fighting in Panjshir with the Mujahideen. In her grief, Fariba has little time or thought for Laila. When Laila's brothers are killed, a messenger comes to inform the family. Laila's mother deteriorates further and now rarely gets out of bed. The household tasks, as well as the care for her mother, fall to Laila. Laila's father, Babi, as she calls him, is a teacher, but he is fired by the Soviets and now works in the local bakery. He is quite loving to Laila and concerned for her education and her future. He points out how much better it has been for women under the Soviet rule. They have legislated a higher marriage age and require women to attend school. In fact, he points out, two-thirds of the students at Kabul University are women. But, the new laws providing equal opportunity to women have also angered those in the rural areas who are bound by their traditions and resent having the Soviets tell them how to treat their women.

Babi takes Laila and Tariq on a day-long trip to Bamiyan to expose them to the heritage and rich culture of their country. On their way, they pass the varied Afghanistan landscape of mountains and deserts. They pass wheat fields, Koochi nomads, and burnt-out Soviet tanks. Laila realizes that the war has been going on around her while Kabul seems to be mostly at peace. When they arrive in Bamiyan, Babi points out Shahr-e-Zohak, or the Red City, built nine hundred years earlier and destroyed by Genghis Khan, evidence of the continuous plight of Afghanistan as a country that has suffered many invasions. He takes them to the two Buddhas, two thousand-year-old statues that served as a home to up to five thousand Buddhist monks and as a sanctuary to travelers. They see the rich Bamiyan countryside, fertile and prosperous, from the height of the Buddhas. As they look out over the countryside, Babi tells Laila that he dreams of moving to America, someplace near the sea, to open an

> The Koochi are the largest group of nomads in Afghanistan. They are Pashtuns and speak Pashto. In Pashto, Koochi means nomad. The Koochi, as do the other nomadic groups, raise livestock, particularly sheep and goats. For more about Koochi nomads, and especially the women, see Ghazi-Walid Falah and Caroline Rose Nagel's book, *Geographies of Muslim Women: Gender, Religion, and Space.* For a discussion of the condition of Koochi nomads forced into refugee camps in Pakistan and elsewhere, especially following Afghanistan's devastating drought beginning in 1998, see Diana Davis's article "How Can We Be Koochi?"

Afghan restaurant that can be a center for the Afghan community in exile and to send Laila to school. They know that Laila's mother will never leave Afghanistan, and Laila worries about leaving Tariq. It is not long after this trip, in April 1988, that Babi comes home announcing that the Soviets have signed a treaty and will be leaving Afghanistan over the next nine months.

In 1989, the last of the Soviets leave and Kabul celebrates and looks forward to the new Islamic State of Afghanistan. The victorious Mujahideen is made up of factions of Pashtuns, Tajiks, Hazaras, and Pashtuns with Arab connections. The plans are for a shared government gradually leading to democratic elections. Laila's mother is revived and she plans a big party, but just as the party disintegrates into fighting over politics and ethnic loyalties, so does the new government of Afghanistan. Soon, the bombs are falling on Kabul, and instead of being outside the fighting, Kabul is the center of the conflict. Meanwhile, Laila and Tariq, now fourteen and sixteen, have fallen in love and their actions threaten to cross the lines of accepted behavior. Laila is warned by her mother to be careful. When the fighting in Kabul begins, however, Laila's mother returns to her bed and no longer pays close attention to Laila.

As the year progresses, Kabul is in a state of chaos. The various warring parties commit atrocities against each other and the civilian population, and bombs fall on Kabul. Laila stops attending school and is taught by her father instead. She spends more time with Tariq until the day he tells her that his family is leaving for Peshawar. He wants her to go with him and tells her that he wants to marry her. Although Laila wants to go with him she cannot abandon her father. As more and more of their neighbors leave Kabul, and militia men and other strangers move into the abandoned homes, Laila's father finally convinces his wife that they should leave as well. But as they are in the process of packing up the house, it is hit by a shell. Laila is blown away from the house and falls unconscious after slamming against a wall. Both of her parents are killed in the blast.

Rasheed rescues Laila from the rubble of her house and she is nursed by Mariam. Shortly after she is able to leave her bed and participate in day-to-day life, a visitor comes to tell Laila that Tariq has died, the victim of a bomb blast. Before many days have passed, it becomes clear to Mariam that Rasheed intends to marry Laila. Mariam is devastated, but when Rasheed asks her to ask Laila for him, she does, and Laila says yes. Laila has become aware that she is pregnant with Tariq's child and she knows marriage is the only option for her at this time. This baby, along with the few books that Rasheed grabbed from the rubble of her house, will be all she has to link her to Tariq and her past.

Mariam keeps her distance from Laila whose marriage to Rasheed is the latest in a long string of humiliations for her. Mariam begins to soften toward her, however, when Laila's baby turns out to be a girl and Laila loses favor with Rasheed. Mariam begins to pay attention to the new baby and soon bonds with her and then with Laila. Laila plans an escape and systematically steals money from Rasheed. However, the latest regime in Afghanistan is hard on women. They are not allowed to travel alone or to be out on the streets unaccompanied by a male family member. When Laila, Mariam, and Aziza (Laila's daughter) attempt to escape, they find a man they believe will help them. However, he takes their money and turns them in to the police. They are returned to their home and Rasheed punishes them by locking Laila and Aziza into a room without fresh air, food, or water. Aziza nearly dies from dehydration before Rasheed lets them out again.

As the Taliban come to power, Laila is again pregnant. By the time she needs to go to the hospital, only one hospital in Kabul will take women. It is horribly understaffed and lacking any of the necessary medicines or equipment. Laila must have a cesarean section, and she must have it without anesthetics or antibiotics. She and the new baby, Zalmai, a boy and the apple of his father's eye, are lucky to survive the ordeal.

A severe drought begins in 1998 and continues into 2000. The family is living on very little, but when Rasheed's shop burns down, starvation becomes a real possibility. Mariam decides to call her father for the first time since she left on her wedding day more than two decades ago, but when she locates someone who knows her father, she discovers that he has been dead for thirteen years. After selling everything and still having no food to feed her children, Laila is forced to take Aziza to an orphanage. This is the same orphanage with the same director as the character in *The Kite Runner*. Zaman's glasses are still broken from the beating he received from Farid.

Because the Taliban do not allow women out without a male relative, Laila must depend on Rasheed to accompany her to the orphanage to visit Aziza. When he decides he cannot do this anymore, Laila must figure out how to do this on her own. It is difficult and dangerous, and she experiences questions and beatings. After one trip to the orphanage, Laila returns home to find Tariq waiting outside the house. Laila is amazed and overjoyed to see Tariq. Mariam and Zalmai go upstairs, leaving Laila to talk with Tariq. Zalmai is jealous of his mother's distraction and tells his father about the visitor. Rasheed goes into a murderous rage, and as his hands are around Laila's neck, her body and face begin showing signs of lifelessness. Mariam gets a shovel from the shed and beats Rasheed over the head. She kills him. Mariam tries to comfort Laila, telling her that she will think of a way to take care of this new crisis. The next morning, Mariam has made her decision. She tells Laila to "Think like a mother, Laila jo. Think like a mother. I am" (319). Mariam has decided to sacrifice herself for the well-being of Laila and the children; they have been her loving family. She sends Laila off to visit Aziza, and, by the time Laila is back, Mariam has disappeared.

Mariam goes to the Walayat Women's Prison. Hosseini describes the conditions of the prison: the women wear their burqas because of the lack of privacy and the unwanted stares of the prison guards. They are given no food and are dependent on food being brought in from outside. Although Mariam is in prison for murder, the other women are primarily in prison for trying to run away. They look up to Mariam and help her with food. Mariam is tried with no legal counsel, no public hearing, no cross-examination, and no possibility of appeal. Her hearing is fifteen minutes long. Mariam is taken to Ghazi Stadium. The Talib guard offers her some comfort, telling her that it is not shameful to be afraid, but Mariam does not break down at the moment of execution. She imagines the pleasant moments of her life, the moments during

The Co-operation Centre for Afghanistan reported that there are several prisons with hundreds of women. In Kandahar at Karez Bazaar from 400 to 500 women are kept as prisoners. The prison at Welayat-e-Kabul has about sixty women prisoners. Women prisoners receive two loaves of bread a day and are not allowed access to their relatives.

From Rosemarie Skaine, The Women of Afghanistan
Under the Taliban.

Ghazi Stadium, the national stadium of Afghanistan, first opened in 1923 and seats 25,000 people. Buzkashi and other events were held here. Under the Taliban, it was the site of public executions as well as soccer games. Today it is still used for soccer.

which she experienced love and beauty. Hosseini writes that "One last time, Mariam did as she was told" (329).

The last section of the novel focuses on Laila, Tariq, and the children. They go to Murree, a tourist site in Pakistan where Tariq had been living and working before coming back to Kabul to find Laila. Aziza is finally with a father who loves her, but Zalmai has difficulty adjusting and misses Rasheed. They all work together for the hotel until, after September 11, 2001, and the U.S. invasion of Afghanistan, Laila begins to feel that they should return to Kabul to help with the reconstruction. Tariq agrees to return, and they stop in Herat to visit Mariam's birthplace and to see whether anyone there remembers her.

Back in Kabul, both children are in school. Laila and Tariq work with Zaman at the orphanage. Laila teaches and Tariq helps with repairs and other reconstruction work. Laila is pregnant again, but all this happiness is overshadowed by the return of the warlords to Kabul and evidence that Afghanistan continues to be an unstable country.

## THE CITY AND THE COUNTRYSIDE: SETTING IN *A THOUSAND SPLENDID SUNS*

Hosseini's novel takes place across Afghanistan, but primarily in the cities of Herat and Kabul. Mariam grows up just outside the fictional village of Gul Daman on the outskirts of Herat. Her home is set apart from the village and is alongside a stream. The rural simplicity of her life in the one-room *kolba* is quite different from that of her father and his large family. Hosseini provides ample description of the flowers and tree-lined streets of Herat. Kabul and Herat are directly east and west from each other in the northern half of Afghanistan. Between them is a fairly impassable mountainous region that includes Hazarajat. Herat is near Afghanistan's borders with Iran and Turkmenistan, and Kabul is closer to Afghanistan's border with Pakistan.

Mariam takes the bus from Herat to Kabul with Rasheed. The farthest she has been from her home until this time is her walk to Herat to see her father. At that time she was overwhelmed with the bustle of the big city. Kabul is the largest city in Afghanistan as well as the capital with more than 2 million people (as of 2003). Herat is probably the fifth largest city in Afghanistan with a 2003 population of 171,500. There is no direct route from Herat to Kabul. It is likely that they traveled southwest to Kandahar and then back north to Kabul, approximately 1,090 kilometers or 680 miles. It takes Mariam and Rasheed until the evening of the next day to reach Kabul by bus. Whichever route they took, Mariam would have been amazed by the activity and the crowds in Kabul.

Later in the novel, Babi takes Laila and Tariq to Bamiyan, a province in the area known as Hazarajat because it has been the homeland to the Hazaras. It is there that the famous Buddha statues were located and the caves still remain. Babi's trip with Tariq and Laila predates the Taliban, and so the Buddhas are standing, and Babi describes them and relates some of their history and purpose. On the way there, Laila notices the vestiges of war. Luckily for them, Kabul has not been at the center of the Soviet and Mujahideen conflict. All that changes after the Soviets withdraw and the different factions fight for control of the capital city.

Tariq and his family emigrate from Afghanistan to Pakistan. When he returns for Laila, and after the death of Rasheed and the disappearance of Mariam into the prison, Tariq, Laila, and the children move to Murree, a popular tourist town in the Rawalpindi district and not far from Islamabad in Pakistan. This little town seems to be an anomaly in this novel of war-torn cities, refugee camps, and prisons; it is a little paradise, with a kind hotel manager, television (on which they see news of the September 11 attacks), a population with the time and luxury to be tourists (not just surviving from day to day), and a lovely and peaceful surrounding. Laila chooses to give up this oasis to return to Kabul.

---

Mariam grew up in a *kolba*. Hosseini describes it when Laila returns to Herat to pay homage to Mariam. Common domestic dwellings in northwestern Afghanistan include buildings made with mud and brick. Furnishings are minimal, and there is usually a common room where the whole family will sleep. Mattresses are laid out at night and are folded and moved to a corner during the day. Mariam and Rasheed live in a multistory house in Kabul and sleep on beds. Mariam's father lives in a large compound style house in Herat. (See Melvin Ember and Carol R. Ember, *Countries and Their Cultures*, and Timothy Gall and Gale Research Inc., *Worldmark Encyclopedia of Cultures and Daily Life*.)

Through this variety of settings, cities of different sizes, rural countryside, the apparent bounty of the Bamiyan landscape, hustle and bustle of Kabul's shop-lined Chicken Street, and the Titanic City bazaar in the dry riverbed of the Kabul River, Hosseini provides a rich setting for his novel. At the same time, he informs and educates his reader about the diversity in Afghanistan.

## THE CHARACTERS OF *A THOUSAND SPLENDID SUNS*

The narrative of *A Thousand Splendid Suns* alternates between Mariam's story and Laila's story. The novel opens with five-year-old Mariam waiting for her father, Jalil, and the climax occurs with her death. In the opening chapters of the novel, the reader is introduced to Mariam's family and close neighbors. Mariam seems to be a happy child, eagerly awaiting the days of her father's visits, an eagerness that is painful to her mother. Nana is Mariam's mother. She was working in Jalil's household until she was forced to leave after becoming pregnant with his child. Nana has remained unmarried. As a young girl, Nana was engaged to be married, but before the engagement could be finalized, she fell victim to a Jinn. This is how she describes it in the novel, and it is probably some kind of seizure. This malady made her unfit for marriage, and her bitterness, which has grown over the years, has only increased further with Jalil's rejection.

Although Nana has been forced from her employment in Jalil's household, Jalil provides for her and Mariam. He operates the local cinema, and it is the lure of this cinema that leads to the initial crisis in *A Thousand Splendid Suns*. All Mariam wants for her birthday is to go to the cinema with her father; he is unwilling to be seen with her in public, but nonetheless promises to meet Mariam the next day on her birthday—a promise he does not keep. Mariam is strong-willed, and when Jalil does not appear, she goes against her mother's wishes and walks into Herat to find him. Although she is not allowed into his house, she refuses to leave. Later, when she turns against her father, it takes a state of desperation for her to attempt to talk with him. Her father, however weak and self-indulgent, is indeed kind. He loves Mariam and has not failed to provide for her immediate needs and within the manner acceptable to his family and to the culture. He tries repeatedly to reconnect with Mariam after she leaves, even driving to Kabul to find her. He leaves a small sentimental gift for Mariam with one of the villagers in Gul Daman that Laila later retrieves after both Jalil and Mariam are dead.

Jalil's family is large. He has ten children from his three wives, and Mariam makes eleven. The members of Jalil's household include Muhsin, the eldest son, and two other sons, Farhad and Ramin. The boys deliver supplies to Nana and Mariam for their father. Nana usually treats them poorly, even throwing rocks at them. His daughters include Saideh and Naheed and eight-year-old Niloufer, who speaks with Mariam during the few days she stays with her father. We read that Saideh and Naheed are allowed to go to school. Mariam is envious of them. Jalil's three wives are Afsoon, Khadija, and Nargis. Jalil's family represents a middle ground in Afghan culture, with Rasheed and Laila's father, perhaps, representing two opposite extremes. Jalil is the public presence of his family and he has three wives as allowed by Islam. However, the wives are not submissive or intimidated by Jalil. In fact, it appears as though it is Jalil who is intimidated by the wives and who must submit to their will. Jalil must move Nana out of the house, and Mariam may not live with him because this is what the wives wish. Their actions are socially acceptable, whereas it may not be socially acceptable and also cause for gossip if Jalil were to keep Nana nearby or allow his illegitimate daughter to live with him.

Mariam's friend and mentor from the village of Gul Daman, Mullah Faizullah, is a village elder. He teaches her to read and write and to memorize the Koran. He is one of the only positive relationships that Mariam has as a child. Mullah Faizullah, like Jalil, serves as a counter example to stereotypes associated with Islam and particularly Islam in Afghanistan. Contrary to what we read about conditions for women and girls under the Taliban, Mullah Faizullah is an Islamic teacher who is kind to and supportive of Mariam. In fact, he even attempts to convince Nana to allow Mariam to go to school. "If the girl wants to learn, let her, my dear. Let the girl have an education" (17). Although Mariam never sees him again after leaving for Kabul, Mullah Faizullah clearly has a lasting influence on her. Bibi jo and Habib Khan, a village leader, are two more characters from Mariam's childhood who come from the little village of Gul Daman.

Rasheed is the suitor chosen for Mariam by Jalil's wives. The first time Mariam sees Rasheed is when she sees his reflection along with her own during the engagement ceremony. Rasheed takes Mariam away from Herat forever. Except for a few tender moments, Hosseini does not portray Rasheed with any positive strokes. The tender moments are transient. His one redeeming feature is that he adores Zalmai, his son with Laila, his second wife. Even this adoration for Zalmai is tainted by the fact that Rasheed is so brutal to Laila, Aziza, and Mariam. Rasheed was married before his marriage to Mariam, but both his first wife and son have died. Mariam feels sorrow for him because of this. She imagines that Rasheed's sorrow is something that will create a bond between them; she "feels for the first time a kinship

A mullah is a term from the Persian meaning a leader or learned man. As used in this novel, the mullah is a preacher or spiritual adviser within the Sunni Islam tradition. Mullahs also teach in elementary schools. They preside at ceremonies, including weddings, births, and funerals. They are not clergy, because the Sunni tradition does not recognize the need for an intermediary between the supplicant and God. Individuals may attend schools and during his reign, King Amanullah established state-sponsored schools. In *A Thousand Splendid Suns*, Mullah Faizullah teaches Mariam privately and is Mariam's closest friend and only mentor. In *The Kite Runner*, Amir's father consistently refers to the mullahs in a derogatory manner. (See Ludwig Adamec, *Historical Dictionary of Afghanistan*, and John Esposito, *The Oxford Encyclopedia of the Modern Islamic World*.)

with her husband. She [tells] herself that they would make good companions after all."

Rasheed brings Mariam to Kabul from Herat and it is through him that she becomes acquainted with Laila. Laila, born in 1978, is an infant when Mariam is a newlywed. She is the daughter of Fariba and Hakim. Hakim is a schoolteacher and he and Fariba have a modern, Western-style household. Hakim is mild mannered and is devoted to Laila. Fariba is easygoing and attached to her sons, who after the Soviet occupation leave to join the Mujahideen. When Mariam goes to her neighborhood's communal tandoor, Fariba befriends her. They are both wearing a *hijab*, a headscarf, in this case, probably covering their hair and necks, but not their faces. Fariba introduces herself to Mariam and extends an open invitation to her to visit and have tea. Later, Rasheed forbids Mariam from associating with Fariba. He points her out as a bad example. He accuses Hakim of having lost control of his wife, of spoiling his own "*nang* and *namoos*," his honor and pride, by letting others see his wife. Rasheed intends to have Mariam wear a burqa, a complete head-to-toe covering, including hands and face, when she is out of the house.

Rasheed may despise Hakim for his education, but it is through Hakim that Hosseini colors his novel with details about the history and culture of Afghanistan. Again, through one of his characters, Hosseini provides some balance to the widely publicized news about present-day Afghanistan's low literacy rate, poverty, and desolation. Hakim shares with Laila and Tariq the richness of Afghanistan's cultural past, and in so doing, shares it with Hosseini's readers as well. When the shells destroy Laila's house, killing her parents, her father's library is also destroyed and remnants of Afghanistan's history along with it.

Hakim and Fariba's sons, Ahmad and Noor, are killed fighting the Soviet Union. The death of her sons sends Fariba to bed. Like many others in Afghanistan, Hakim, Laila, and Fariba had looked forward to the defeat of the Soviet Union by the Mujahideen. Even Fariba gets out of bed and celebrates with her neighbors when this happens. However, as the factions begin to fight over Kabul, Fariba returns to bed and the bloodshed is even worse than before. Ultimately, Hakim and Fariba die in the civil war that follows the withdrawal of the Soviet Union.

Laila has a privileged childhood, especially when compared with Mariam's. Although she suffers from the neglect of her mother, she has the love of her father and she has freedom to attend school and to play and to roam with her friends, including several girls her own age and Tariq. While Mariam is described as plain, Laila is remarkably beautiful. But Laila is not spoiled and must do much of the work around the house and prepare meals for her father. By the time her mother and father are killed in the bomb blast, she has lost her brothers and several of her girl-friends to the wars. She has also been separated from her childhood sweetheart, Tariq. In the wake of the civil war, Tariq's family decides to leave for Pakistan. It is his imminent departure that rushes the two youngsters into sexual intimacy, and Laila is pregnant when she accepts Rasheed's marriage proposal.

Laila gives birth first to Aziza, who is really Tariq's child, and then, to the great happiness of Rasheed, a son, Zalmai. Even when famine strikes and the family is destitute, Rasheed finds ways to indulge Zalmai. But, as conditions worsen, Rasheed insists that they send Aziza to an orphanage. Hosseini depicts the same orphanage and reintroduces the character Zaman, the orphanage director, from *The Kite Runner*. It is

---

Mujahideen are Afghan resistance fighters, waging a holy war against a non-Islamic government. The Mujahideen in Afghanistan were a loose alliance of seven Sunni groups and another alliance of eight Shi'a groups. The Sunni groups had the support of Pakistan. After the with-drawal of Soviet troops, the Mujahideen took over Kabul and declared Afghanistan an Islamic state. Commander Ahmad Shah Massoud was the primary leader in Kabul until the Taliban captured it in 1996. (See Amin Saikal et al., *Modern Afghanistan: A History of Struggle and Survival*, and Ludwig Adamec, *Historical Dictionary of Afghanistan*.)

after visiting Aziza at the orphanage that Laila finds Tariq miraculously waiting for her in front of Rasheed's house. His return leads to the second pivotal moment in Mariam's life, the first culminating in the suicide of her mother. When Rasheed learns of Tariq's return, he viciously attacks Laila, nearly killing her. In an effort to save her, Mariam kills Rasheed, and this leads to her fateful decision to urge Laila, Tariq, and the children to flee while she stays to take the consequences. They escape back to Pakistan and settle at the resort in Murree, Pakistan, run by the kind Sayeed. They later return to Kabul where Tariq works with Zaman to rebuild the school and Laila teaches the orphans.

## THE PLIGHT OF WOMEN AND THE HISTORY OF AFGHANISTAN: THEMES IN *A THOUSAND SPLENDID SUNS*

In *A Thousand Splendid Suns*, Hosseini tells the stories of Mariam and Laila, but he also tells the story of Afghanistan. Through his storytelling, he describes a changing Afghanistan, a country of social, cultural, and economic diversity, a country that has undergone destructive political upheaval, a country of beauty and history, and a country of desolation and deprivation. Through Babi, Laila's schoolteacher father, Hosseini informs the reader about the history and literary traditions of Afghanistan. Babi takes Laila and Tariq to see the two giant Buddhas in Bamiyan. Many readers may be familiar with the story of these ancient structures, but Hosseini makes sure that the reader knows that there was a living history associated with these statues. They are not mysterious remnants of the past like the Sphinx; their purpose and use are known. They represent religious tolerance, hospitality to the stranger, and a place of learning. Babi also talks about Shahr-e-Zohak, the Red City, and it is through Babi that we hear about the Persian poetic tradition of Afghanistan. When a shell tragically strikes Laila's house during the civil war, she loses not only her family, but also her father's library. This loss symbolizes the loss of Afghanistan's literary tradition, which Babi, through his love and devotion to the poets, had preserved through the occupation and the civil war. We read that the pages of Khalili, Pajwak, Ansari, Haji Dehqan, Ashraqi, Beytaab, Hafez, Jami, Nizami, Rumi, Khayyám, and Beydel are going up in flames.

Most North Americans know about Afghanistan from what we have heard about the Taliban during the 1990s and from what we hear about the conflict and efforts to establish a new state in the early twenty-first century. Hosseini seems to want his readers to know about an Afghanistan that was productive and flourishing. From the heights of the

Buddhas, Laila and Tariq see a Bamiyan with "lush farming fields," wheat, alfalfa, potatoes, poplars bordering fields and lining streets, streams, irrigation ditches, rice paddies, and barley fields; they see tea shops, barbers, small shops, horses, sheep, and cows. Babi tells them, "see your country's heritage" and urges them to "learn of its rich past" (134). Earlier in the novel, Hosseini describes Mariam's first visit to Herat. Mariam sees a bustling city, with cypress-lined streets and flower-beds; people walk the streets and the street markets are abundant. Not only is the city beautiful, but it also is safe and friendly even for such a young girl as Mariam. Although she walks alone and is clearly of mea-ger means, no one points or shouts at her, and no one questions the fact that she is walking alone or suggests that she has anything of which she should be ashamed. In fact, a taxi driver picks her up and takes her to her destination. This is in stark contrast to Mariam's experience in the Kabul market and her sense of safe anonymity within her burqa, and to Laila's terrifying trips to visit her daughter Aziza in the orphanage.

The story of Afghanistan includes the story of the role and place of women in Afghan society. Hosseini touches on this in *The Kite Runner*, but he has clearly dedicated himself to examining the condition of women in this novel. Laila is the beloved daughter of her father, but her mother focuses primarily on Laila's brothers. Laila is all but forgotten in her mother's grief for the loss of her two sons. Mariam, in contrast to Laila, lives in poverty but has the rough love of her mother and the apparent doting of her father. Both girls' lives change abruptly and clearly for the worst when they become connected to Rasheed through marriage. They each enjoy a brief honeymoon period with their husband, but they are ruled by his wishes and desires and defy him at great risk to their well-being, and in Laila's case, the well-being of her children. It may pass through the mind of the reader to wonder whether Hosseini has over-stated his case. Rasheed's treatment of Mariam predates the Soviet inva-sion and the civil war, and his relationship with both Laila and Mariam predates the Taliban. At no time does it appear that Laila or Mariam have any legal rights. But Hosseini carefully portrays both Laila, whose parents raised her with a greater sense of entitlement and privilege, and Mariam, whose mother taught her to endure by taking control of the conditions under which they lived to the extent that they possibly could. When Mariam finally softens to the infant Aziza and reconciles herself to the presence of Laila in her household, they become allies.

Rasheed's marriage to Mariam and Laila is one representation of marriage in Afghanistan. However, Laila's parents married for love. They were cousins, which is common and even preferred in Afghanistan, but their marriage was not arranged. Laila's father is in the weaker position in the marriage, with the mother influencing decisions and the tenor of domestic life. Nana, Mariam's mother, had been engaged to a young man in the more typical manner of an arranged marriage. Her illness, perhaps epilepsy, or as she calls it, her Jinn, became apparent before the engagement was finalized, and the suitor's family abandoned her. This abandonment was a stigma that Nana carried with her to her death. Mariam's father, Jalil, has several wives in the same manner as Rasheed. The impression given is that his is a domestically peaceful arrangement. Jalil and his wives are compatible and all make decisions together. The wives together are able to influence Jalil to marry off Mariam, a decision that he accepts but soon regrets. Laila and Tariq are perhaps the fairy tale romance of the novel. They are neither cousins nor even of the same ethnic background. They are childhood friends who drift into a romantic attachment at an early age. Presumably parted for life, they find each other again, older, wiser, and painfully more experienced. Despite their experiences, they are resilient enough to love each other and to form a loving family for the children. The novel ends with the knowledge that another child is on the way.

Mariam makes the ultimate sacrifice for the woman and children who have become her family and for the relationship she sees that Tariq and Laila might have. Although her final act is tragic, it is also heroic and a choice that she makes. Mariam lives out the final days of her life in the Walayat Women's Prison. To the women in the prison, many of whom are imprisoned for attempting to run away from their husbands, Mariam, who has killed her husband, is a hero. She is honored and cared for by her cellmates and loved by their children until her final day. It is well to recognize that Hosseini's characters are neither passive nor helpless, but they are abused and their lives are made tragic by social and religious mores and the political restrictions placed on them and the lack of any kind of support afforded them. Hosseini strengthens his case in pointing out the hypocrisy behind laws put into place by the Taliban who forbade women from working outside the home even when no males in the family could support them, who prevented females from attending school, and who endangered the lives of women and children by limiting the availability of health care for women to one severely understaffed and unfunded hospital in Kabul.

Finally, Hosseini provides insight into the daily life within Afghanistan both in the city and in the rural areas. We hear about how meals are prepared and about the foods that are eaten; we learn about the interaction between males and females in public and within the home; we learn about celebrations and festivals, Tajiks and Pashtuns, dialects and languages.

Hosseini ends *A Thousand Splendid Suns* on a note of hope. There is no celebration—but there is hope and a desire for betterment. Interestingly, both of Hosseini's novels end with a focus on children. Laila and Tariq are working with the orphanage in Kabul, and Hosseini ends his first novel, *The Kite Runner*, with news of the construction of a new pediatric unit near the Afghanistan–Pakistan border. Perhaps Hosseini is suggesting that it is with the children that there is a chance for a better more humane Afghanistan, and so his characters focus on the well-being of the children, the most vulnerable in times of war and famine, acting to protect them, nurture and care for them, and keep them safe.

## DISCUSSION QUESTIONS

- Hosseini tells a compelling story, and, in the process, teaches the reader about Afghanistan. How has your perception of Afghanistan changed since reading this book?

- Laila's father is a teacher. He serves two different purposes in the novel: he is a male who is counter to the stereotypical male Muslim and he provides his children, and thus the reader, with history lessons. How does his character defy stereotyping? What are some of the history lessons we learn from him?

- Describe the character of Mullah Faizullah. Similarly to Laila's father, he both presents a countermodel to stereotypes and he provides us with insight into religious beliefs and practices. What are your impressions of Mullah Faizullah and what does he tell us about Islamic beliefs and practices?

- When Mariam travels to Herat she travels through the countryside and across the city by herself. Compare this with circumstances in Kabul when she first arrives, and later after the Soviets have withdrawn.

- Through his storytelling, Hosseini describes the social stratification of Afghanistan. Think about the different characters in the novel, from Mariam and Laila and Nana and Jalil to Rasheed and Tariq and Laila's friends. What do you learn about the social hierarchy and the ethnic divisions in Afghanistan through the characters' relationships and attitudes?

- How do rural and urban living differ one from the other as described by Hosseini?

- Hosseini does not come out and tell us that life in Afghanistan was not always as it is now. How does he work in the details of Afghanistan's varied geography, history, culture, and everyday life without making his novel read like a textbook?

- Can you imagine a story where, following Nana's suicide, Mariam stayed in her own village with Mullah Faizullah or Bibi jo? What elements of Mariam's life might have been different?
- As Afsoon turns the key in the lock of Mariam's bedroom after Mariam learns that she is to be engaged and sent to Kabul the next day, Mariam seems to have lost all agency in her own life. How does this play out through the rest of the novel?
- Hosseini describes his characters through their actions and decisions and words. What kind of a person is Mariam and what events in the novel help us to see her characteristics? Contrast her with Nana, Jalil, and Laila.
- In The Kite Runner, Hassan was always good and Assef was diabolically evil. In A Thousand Splendid Suns the characters are more complex. Talk about some of the characteristics and complexities of the central characters in A Thousand Splendid Suns and compare them with those in The Kite Runner.
- Mariam's decision to never see or speak with Jalil has consequences. What are they?
- Mariam's first impressions of Rasheed are not all bad. Does Rasheed set out to fool her or does Rasheed change?
- Compare the difference between how Mariam's husband lives and how Laila's family—just down the street—lives. In particular, consider the party that Rasheed had when celebrating Mariam's first pregnancy and the party that Laila's family has when the Mujahideen begin to enter Kabul after the fall of the Communist government.
- Mariam's character goes through many changes. Trace those changes from her isolated childhood with her unhappy mother to her family life with Laila and the children.
- Many elements go into setting the scene for Mariam's execution and the conclusion of the novel. How does the execution sum up Mariam's life? If we think of Mariam as a victim, of whom or what is she a victim? In what ways does Mariam defy her victimhood?
- Similarly, Laila becomes an orphan and finds that her only recourse is to marry a controlling abusive husband nearly forty years older than her. How does Hosseini portray Laila as a powerful person despite these overwhelming tragic circumstances?
- What difference does it make that the novel does not end with Mariam's death?

# 5

# TODAY'S ISSUES IN KHALED HOSSEINI'S WORK

Khaled Hosseini's works are built around issues that are of importance in the twenty-first century. Although the issues present in his novels can be seen as particular to the country of Afghanistan, readers can extrapolate from Hosseini's implicit commentary and see how they relate to United States society and culture. Hosseini tucks within the plots and narratives of his two novels events and details that address the state of civil strife and international hegemony in Afghanistan, including the U.S. involvement there beginning in 2001. Through the details of his plots and the interactions of his characters, Hosseini presents problems of racism and ethnocentrism, as well as exile and immigration. Hosseini explores issues of gender equality, gender stereotypes, and domestic abuse. Both novels illustrate to some extent the excesses and abuses of governments, and the novels include references to capital punishment, political and economic injustice, religious freedom, linguistic diversity, literacy and enfranchisement, and familial relationships.

Hosseini's books reflect a wide range of important current events and contemporary issues. Certainly, the wars in Afghanistan are all encompassing in both novels. Hosseini was in the middle of writing

*The Kite Runner* when al-Qaeda operatives committed their suicide attacks on the Pentagon and the twin towers of the World Trade Center on September 11, 2001. The novel appeared two years later, in 2003, with the United States immersed in wars in both Afghanistan and Iraq. Hosseini's American audience was ready to learn about this country. With *The Kite Runner*, Hosseini provides to Western readers historical background to the thirty years of war and instability in that country and an intimate look at Afghanistan's culture and people. With *A Thousand Splendid Suns*, readers learn even more about day-to-day life in Afghanistan, the urban and rural tensions that exist and that have some responsibility for the era of violence and upheaval there, and the devastating nature of each wave of war to Afghanistan's people and culture.

In *A Thousand Splendid Suns*, Laila, Tariq, and family return to Afghanistan after the U.S. invasion with plans to rebuild the country. They work at the orphanage where Aziza stayed during the darkest times of drought and famine, and where *The Kite Runner*'s Sohrab is sent after his parents are murdered. They return there hoping for a new era for Afghanistan; however, the novel's end suggests the instability of the country. Laila observes the transformation of Kabul as residents repair and rebuild, but she also knows that all is not well.

> It slays Laila . . . that the warlords have been allowed back to . . . live in posh homes with walled gardens, that they have been appointed minister of this and deputy minister of that, that they ride with impunity . . . through neighborhoods that they demolished. (363)

Readers coming to the novel know even more than Laila and Tariq. This novel, set in the early twenty-first century, becomes more tragic as the situation in Afghanistan worsens. In early 2009, the state of Afghanistan was increasingly uncertain. U.S. President Barack Obama called for more troops to be sent there and the Taliban continued to create havoc and to try to regain control of the country. Schools have been bombed, including perhaps orphanages like the one described in Hosseini's novels, and readers know that innocent civilians, including women and children, continue to lose their lives as the country remains unstable.

In *The Kite Runner,* Hosseini's story of a troubled father-and-son relationship and friendship, betrayal, and reconciliation takes place within a deeper and more balanced view of a country of which few Americans had much knowledge. Usually, in a time of war, countries vilify and dehumanize their enemies. But Hosseini takes his readers beyond the terrorist camps and *madrassas* to show a country where children fly kites and go to the cinema to see American Westerns. He portrays a man, Amir's father, who is worldly and travels to other countries on business, who builds orphanages, and who cares for friends and acquaintances in need. Amir's father, rather than in thrall to a religious viewpoint, is critical of the mullahs who teach Amir. He tells Amir, "You'll never learn anything of value from those bearded idiots. . . . God help us all if Afghanistan ever falls into their hands" (17).

Hosseini provides an even fuller portrait of Afghanistan in *A Thousand Splendid Suns*, taking the reader deeper into the country's history. He sets the novel in several cities across thirty years of turmoil. The novel takes place not only in Kabul but also in Herat, Bamiyan, and Mariam's small fictional village just outside of Herat. Hosseini fills out the outlines that he provided the reader in *The Kite Runner*, working into his second novel's narrative the history of Afghanistan's long series of conflicts. Through the character of Laila's schoolteacher-father, the reader receives a history lesson along with Laila and Tariq as Laila's father tells the two children about their heritage.

Finally, with Hosseini's depiction of Herat and Kabul before and during the Soviet invasion, the reader sees a much more modern Afghanistan than that described through media photographs and television coverage. Even so, Hosseini's Afghanistan has a very different social and cultural environment from that of most people living in Europe or the United States. Social restrictions for young people are strong. As a rule, for example, girls and boys do not play together after a certain age without inviting gossip and criticism. Women take their bread to a communal oven for baking and shop at open markets. While Laila and her family live a life that is somewhat closer to one with which Hosseini's Western readers might be familiar, another character, Rasheed, maintains strict gender segregation. When he has a party in honor of Mariam's pregnancy, Mariam must stay apart from the male guests. Laila attends school with her girl friends, but she is not safe walking the streets alone. She and her friends wear Western-style clothing, but Mariam wears more traditional Afghan clothing, including a headscarf as a child, and then the full covering once she is married to Rasheed.

Mariam observes the difference between women in the commercial, more prosperous areas of Kabul compared with those in her poor neighborhood, "These women were . . . modern Afghan women. . . . These women mystified Mariam. They made her aware of her own lowliness, her plain looks, her lack of aspirations, her ignorance of so many things" (68).

Along with the history of Afghanistan, Hosseini also creates characters who provide a range of personalities and types, and who break stereotypes with which readers may come to his novels. Rasheed is a terrible bully and oppressive husband. He certainly fits into the stereotype of the controlling, autocratic husband in a patriarchal society, which is exemplified later in the policies established for women by the Taliban. His character contrasts, however, with Mariam's father who is the head of his household, the breadwinner, but who Hosseini does not describe as in any way dominating his wives. Rasheed also stands in sharp contrast to Laila's father, Babi, and to Tariq who is portrayed as sometimes playful and teasing, but always gentle, loving, patient, and protective. Babi is intimidated by his wife, but more positively, he wants his daughter to be educated and to have a successful professional career. He imagines moving away from Afghanistan to America to open a restaurant or café. He tells Laila, "And you . . . would continue going to school . . . to get you a good education, high school then college" (136).

Babi is a lover of poetry and he serves as a source of information about the cultural history of Afghanistan. He takes Tariq and Laila to Bamiyan to admire the Buddhas, to see the lush and fertile countryside, and to learn something about the greatness of their country. He explains to Laila and Tariq, "I wanted you to . . . see your country's heritage . . . to learn of its rich past" (134). He quotes from the Persian poets and has a large library—all but a few volumes of which are destroyed in the bomb blast that kills him and Laila's mother. As Babi and Laila pack for their departure, Babi grieves for the books he will leave behind. He tells Laila that he never thought he would leave Kabul or abandon his library. Babi's library represents Afghanistan's long tradition of the written word, especially poetry. Through Babi, Hosseini introduces his readers to many Afghan poets, most of whom wrote in Farsi. The bomb that destroys Hosseini's library symbolizes the destruction of Afghan culture that has resulted from the warring and policies of the Soviets, the Mujahideen and the Taliban.

Hassan does not know how to read when he is a servant in the household of Amir and Baba. The United Nations reports that only 28 percent of the population of Afghanistan is literate. This is the lowest literacy rate in the world. United Nations Educational, Scientific, and Cultural Organization (UNESCO) statistics from 2007 show that adult women fifteen years and older have a 12.6 percent literacy rate and men fifteen years and older have a 43.1 percent literacy rate.

Literacy is a theme evident in both novels. It is a significant element in the plot of *The Kite Runner*. Amir exploits his position of authority, even as a young child, by consciously depriving Hassan the opportunity to learn to read, although it is clearly something that Hassan strongly desires. He does so to maintain the imbalance in their relationship. As soon as Hassan is free from his position of servitude in Amir's household, he does learn to read and he makes sure that his own child learns to read. When Hassan reads to Sohrab from the same book that he and Amir used to read together, he does so with the expectation that Sohrab will soon read the book for himself. In his letter he tells Amir, "Sohrab and I still sit under [the pomegranate's] shade and I read to him from the *Shahnamah*. . . . Soon he will be able to read from the book himself" (217). Afghanistan has a desperately low literacy rate. But this is also a serious problem in the United States. Although the United States claims a 99 percent literacy rate, the functional literacy rate, the level necessary to hold most jobs, is most likely much lower than 99 percent. In 2002, the National Center for Education Statistics determined that between 40 and 44 million U.S. adults performed at the lowest literacy levels (Kirsch 41). Of these more than 40 million individuals, 40 to 41 percent were living at or below the federal poverty level compared with 4 to 5 percent of those Americans performing at the highest literacy levels (Kirsch 85). Not surprisingly, those individuals with the lowest literacy rates were the least likely to be employed (Kirsch 87). Although the demands in the United States are different from those in Afghanistan, it is clear that literacy, whether the ability to read or to work with numbers, is required in most societies to rise above a certain socioeconomic level. Keeping a population illiterate is a time-tested way to keep a population subservient.

Similarly to Hassan, Mariam desires an education and it is something that Laila takes for granted (although her father realizes that this is a gift to be valued). Mariam cannot go to school, but the village mullah teaches her to read. Hosseini's mullah counters the representation of an Islam that is oppressive to women. Hosseini describes the seriousness and intensity with which Mariam and Mullah Faizullah approach these lessons, but he also makes clear the meagerness of Mariam's education opportunities.

Although Mariam does not have much, the skills she learns from the supportive mullah keep her from being completely powerless, and her ability to read and recite from the Koran provides her with comfort.

The powerlessness or status of women in Afghanistan has been of great concern to Americans, and Hosseini addresses this directly in *A Thousand Splendid Suns*. He presents multiple aspects of women's experience in Afghanistan at different points in recent history and in rural and urban Afghanistan through the characters of Laila and Mariam, as well as through his more peripheral characters. Hosseini depicts Mariam's narrow range of opportunities living with her single mother. This contrasts sharply with the opportunities available to her father's legitimate children. Mariam cannot go to school, but that is because of her social condition and not because she is a girl. It is also because of her mother's fear of losing her. In fact it is learning about her sisters attending school that raises Mariam's hopes that she might also go to school. Despite pleas from the mullah on Mariam's behalf, her mother is emphatically against it, telling Mariam that it is not her "lot in life. . . . We endure. It's all we have" (18). Nana tells Mariam that the other children will laugh at her and call her *harami* and then tells the mullah, "There is nothing out there for her. Nothing but rejection and heartache" (18).

Although Mariam's life is constrained from the beginning, Laila is raised with the freedom to go to school, to play in the streets with her friends, and even to spend time alone with Tariq, although this begins to inspire gossip. Her life changes drastically after her parents are killed and Rasheed rescues her from the rubble of her house and then marries her. She enjoys a higher status than Mariam in the household because of her youth and because she eventually gives birth to a son. This is yet another sign of the deflated status of women in Afghan society as the birth of a daughter is no cause for celebration. But she, like Mariam, cannot go out alone; she is required by Rasheed, and later the Taliban, to wear the full-length burqa. To contradict her husband or to venture an opinion of her own is to risk severe physical punishment. In contrast, earlier in the novel, when Mariam enters the city of Herat looking for her father, she walks by herself. Readers hear nothing about head-to-toe covering or the need to be accompanied by a male relative until later in the novel when Mariam is married to Rasheed and living in Kabul. In Herat, the wives of Mariam's father have autonomy and a strong voice in family matters. In fact, they are responsible for arranging Mariam's marriage to Rasheed. Neither Laila nor Mariam enjoy anything like this kind of influence in their own marriage to Rasheed.

Women do not figure largely in *The Kite Runner*, but Hosseini does not ignore them. Amir's mother was a professor of literature at the university, and she and Amir's father met when she was a student. Soraya, Amir's wife, wants to be a schoolteacher, but her father wants her to consider returning to Afghanistan to work with a new government. Despite the strict code of behavior required of her by her father, he nonetheless has high expectations for her in terms of her education and choice of profession.

Under the Soviet occupation, the government was supportive of women and ethnic minorities. Both were represented in the government

Mariam has a *nikka*, which is the ceremony in which the marriage contract is signed. It is presided over by a mullah, and there must be two witnesses. Usually these witnesses must be male. The *nikka* is often preceded by an engagement party and the engagement period can be very long. In *The Kite Runner*, Amir and Soraya decide to forgo the engagement period because of Amir's father's weak health. Mariam's abrupt marriage is intended to get her out of her father's house and far away from the family. She is an embarrassment. Her marriage is arranged for the convenience of the family and not with Mariam's interest in mind. Still, the law requires that she go into the wedding voluntarily and so she is asked by the mullah whether or not she agrees to the wedding. Her hesitation makes Jalil and his wives nervous. Typically, marriages are arranged and the bride and groom spend little or no time together before the actual ceremony. Wedding celebrations are segregated by gender. The marriage contract usually includes a bride price given by the husband's family to the bride's family, and also a *mahr*. This is a form of social insurance for the woman in case her husband divorces her. In *Kabul Beauty School*, Deborah Rodriguez describes events surrounding a joyous wedding. In his 2006 dissertation, Mir Hekmatullah Sadat states that during the 1970s and 1980s, under the influence of the Mujahideen, weddings became somber events (195).

and in the professions. Girls were required to attend school, and the veil was discouraged. Babi tells Laila that providing an education for women was the one thing that the Soviets had done right, but ironically, it was also one of the causes for their downfall, "*Of course, women's freedom . . . is also one of the reasons people out there took up arms in the first place*" (italics in original, 121). Through Babi's observation, readers can begin to understand the complicated nature of ruling this wide land with little infrastructure for communication or for the centralized rule of law.

The burqa has become within certain political and social-justice communities (both conservative and liberal) an especially pervasive symbol of the plight of Afghanistan's women under the Taliban and within certain segments of Muslim society. Feminist scholars are starting to question the use of the burqa as a symbol of oppression (Ayotte and Husain; Whitlock). Hosseini examines the complexity of this item of clothing within Muslim culture, and in particular, within Afghanistan's culture. Rasheed requires Mariam to wear the full-length burqa long before the Mujahideen or the Taliban require it. Hosseini first describes how awkward it is for Mariam as she tries it out; it is tight and heavy on her

Women have been at the center of political and civil unrest through-out the twentieth century in Afghanistan. In 1923, under King Ama-nullah, the constitution guaranteed equal rights for women and men. In 1953, as Daoud became prime minister, he encouraged women to participate in the government and workforce. In 1958, an Afghan woman attended the United Nations as a delegate from Afghanistan. In 1959, women began to work in public positions, including the national airline, without wearing veils. New policies encouraged women to work and to feel free to choose for themselves whether or not they would wear a veil. They were allowed to attend univer-sities. In 1964, Afghan women received the right to vote. In 1977, Article 27 of the Afghan Constitution gave all Afghan men and women equal rights before the law. In 1978, civil war broke out, in some part due to the Communist government's emphasis on female literacy. In 1979, the Soviets began to push emancipation for women, including more education opportunities and professional training. This was wel-comed by some and deplored by many. More and more women joined the workforce and especially the professions over the next decade. In 1992, the Communist regime fell. Women continued to work but the government required women to cover their hair, and forbade them to wear makeup or to laugh in public. Conditions worsened going into 1996 and the Mujahideen forces targeted for assassination educated women and women in the professions. In 1993, Afghanistan's Supreme Court declared that women should be completely covered by the veil outside their homes. In 1994, Taliban forces captured Kandahar. They forbade girls to attend school and women to work outside their homes. They captured Herat in 1995 and Kabul in 1996. In 1998, the last major area of Afghanistan, Bamiyan in Hazarajat, fell to the Tali-ban. (See Deborah Ellis, *Women of the Afghan War.*)

head, she cannot see clearly, and she trips over the hem. But later, Mariam finds it comforting and a sign that her husband wants her to be protected, "Inside it, she was an observer, buffered from the scrutinizing eyes of strangers" (66). Laila also sees her burqa as something that pro-tects her and provides anonymity when she is out in the street. This item of clothing is a factor in Mariam and Laila's daily existence but not threatening to their immediate well-being as is Rasheed's socially con-doned brutality, their inability to provide for their families, or their lack of access to health care for themselves and the children.

The issue of health care, especially for women, is apparent to a great extent in *A Thousand Splendid Suns,* and to a somewhat lesser extent in *The Kite Runner.* In *The Kite Runner,* Amir's mother dies in childbirth. The fact of her death in this way, despite her relative wealth and privilege, underscores the fragility of life and lack of adequate health care available even in the city and during the relatively prosperous times in Kabul before the Soviet invasion. When Laila is ready to give birth to her son in *A Thousand Splendid Suns,* only one hospital in all of Kabul serves women. This hospital is severely short of staff and lacking in medicine and anesthetic. It seems extreme to portray a cesarean section without anesthetic, but this is historically correct. Kabul had only one hospital for women, few doctors were working there, and they had little or no medicine or means to anesthetize their patients. In her 2000 book, *Women of the Afghan War,* written while the Taliban were still in power, Deborah Ellis wrote of the health care available to women.

> The war and the chaos that comes with it has crippled the health-care delivery system. . . . Women who are trained and could be of use are largely forced to remain at home. Although some women are permitted to provide health care for other women, the hospitals and clinics set aside for female patients are few and ill equipped. (97)

She continued, "The rate of mothers who die while giving birth is the second highest in the world, after Sierra Leone. . . . Almost all births are home deliveries, without trained medical personnel being there" (97). Furthermore, she noted that 70 percent of those suffering from tuberculosis are women and that many patients are tortured by the guards and, as a result of this mistreatment, suffer broken bones and severe burns. Ellis also cited examples of husbands being beaten for trying to take their wives to a hospital.

Two years later, Hafizullah Emadi wrote in her book *Repression, Resistance, and Women in Afghanistan,* "Gender ideology has greatly affected the status of women's health. There are a limited number of health centers in the capital of every province, and women are generally neglected by their husbands and excluded from health care. . . . Even in cases of emergency, medical treatment is conducted in absentia when the medical doctor is a man and the patient is a woman" (Emadi, 47).

As discussed above, issues of gender and ethnic discrimination are strong themes in both of Hosseini's novels. When following the story of Amir and Hassan, it is easy to recognize parallels between the treatment

> Zora Rasekh writes in her chapter on public heath in *Women for Afghan Women,*
>
>> Of all the factors that have led to the failure of the health system in Afghanistan, the Taliban regime bears the greatest share of guilt, specifically in the areas of women's and children's health. In January 1997, Taliban officials announced a policy of segregating men and women into separate hospitals. (177)
>
> She cites that they reserved one hospital to serve a half-million women in Kabul. The Taliban also prevented women from working in any of the health care fields. According to Physicians for Human Rights, the Taliban later relented on this policy due to international pressure. Rasekh writes that the Taliban "reopened a few hospitals for women, and female medical personnel were allowed to return to their jobs" (177).

of the Hazaras in Afghanistan and America's history of slavery and the continued limited opportunities for education and social advancement for many African Americans, Latinos, recent immigrant populations, and other ethnic minority groups. American slaveholders often thought of their human property as part of the family, but as property nonetheless. Black and white children may have been nursed by the same women and might have grown up playing together, but at a certain point, it was clear that only one of the children would grow up with privilege and opportunities, while the other would remain a slave, only welcomed through the back door if inside the house at all.

In *The Kite Runner*, Baba grows up "like a brother" to Ali, and Amir grows up "like a brother" to Hassan. Hassan's tasks include ironing Amir's clothes, preparing and serving his breakfast, and making sure that Amir's school materials are ready. When Amir leaves with his father for school, Hassan leaves with his father for the market. Hassan is loyal and devoted to Amir no matter how Amir treats him. Amir, with his jealousies and insecurities, taunts Hassan and fails to stand up for him. Amir refuses to teach Hassan to read and mocks him for his inability to do so.

> That Hassan would grow up illiterate like Ali and most Hazaras had been decided the minute he had been born . . . after all, what use did a servant have for the written word? . . . My favorite part of reading to Hassan was when we came across a big word that he didn't know. I'd tease him, expose his ignorance. (28)

Hassan is the more noble and compassionate of the two; he has intelligence and athletic ability, but none of this will change his status within Pashtun-dominated Afghanistan. Additionally, just as it was common for slaveholders to father children with their slave women, Amir's father has fathered Hassan with Ali's wife. But this does not advance Hassan out of his state of servitude. "In the end, I was a Pashtun and he was a Hazara, I was Sunni and he was Shi'a, and nothing was ever going to change that. Nothing" (25).

Amir reads for the first time of the mistreatment of the Hazara in a dusty book, written by an Iranian, that he finds in his father's library. Amir is "stunned to find an entire chapter on Hazara history." He discovers through the book that the Pashtuns "had persecuted and oppressed the Hazaras. It said the Hazaras had tried to rise against the Pashtuns in the nineteenth century, but the Pashtuns had 'quelled them with unspeakable violence'" (9).

Hazara slavery was officially ended by decree in 1921 and by the Afghan constitution in 1923. This had only a marginal effect on the well-being of the Hazara in Afghanistan, however, because at the same time, there was an effort to unite the country and move away from tribalism. This has been described as Pashtun nationalism rather than Afghan nationalism. Under Mahmud Tarzi, there was an official effort to make Pashto the official language of Afghanistan rather than Farsi, or its Afghan counterpart, Dari. In his book *The Hazaras of Afghanistan: An Historical, Cultural, Economic, and Political Study*, Sayed Askar Mousavi writes that Mahmud Tarzi believed that "Afghanistan must have its own unique language in order to preserve its independence and sovereignty, especially from its neighbour, Iran" (157). Hazara were Farsi speakers

The Hazara are the third largest ethnic group in Afghanistan, making up about 9 percent of the population. They are primarily Shi'a Muslims and, again, are in the minority with regard to their religious practices. The Sunnis make up 80 percent of the population and the Shi'a Muslims make up about 19 percent of the population of Afghanistan. The Hazara have been discriminated against throughout the twentieth century. King Amanullah abolished slavery in Afghanistan in 1929, a law that chiefly benefited the Hazara. The new constitution, written in 2004, again abolishes slavery, and once again, this law primarily affects the Hazara who were the group most likely to be enslaved within Afghanistan. (See Kathryn M. Coughlin, *Muslim Cultures Today: A Reference Guide*.)

and were among the groups most suppressed during this period of nationalization from the 1930s until the Soviet invasion. Mousavi cites examples of Pashtun oppression of the Hazara. He quotes a common Hazara proverb that translates as "even a Pashtun dog has a protector, but not a Hazara" (160). Mousavi uses two quotations to illustrate the continued low status of the Hazara in Afghanistan; one from the 1890s describes the Hazara as doing the "hardest, dirtiest, and most menial work . . . there is scarcely a house without its Hazara servant, in the form of slaves, stablemen, etc." The other from the 1980s similarly describes the state of the Hazara: "Throughout the past years [before the 1978 coup d'état] the most difficult and lowest paid jobs, poverty, illiteracy, social and nationalist discrimination were the lot of the Hazara people" (162).

The Hazara not only are ethnic and linguistic minorities within Afghanistan, but as described in Amir's history book, also are religious minorities. Mousavi writes that even into the 1970s "the killing of Hazaras was declared by Sunni Pashtun clerics as an accepted and sanctified means of gaining God's favor and securing for oneself a place in Heaven" (Mousavi, 162). During the government of the communist People's Democratic Party of Afghanistan (PDPA), the climate changed for the Hazara as both the prime minister and deputy prime minster were Hazara. Through its constitution, the PDPA did not differentiate among tribes, language, or religion. Because of this, the Hazara fared much better under the PDPA than under previous Afghan governments.

Later in the 1990s, after the withdrawal of the Soviet Union and the fall of Najibullah and the PDPA government, Hazaras made up possibly half the population of Kabul and held most of the western portion of that city. The Hazara were excluded from the new Mujahideen government and thus took up arms against the ruling faction in the civil war that brought bombs down on the civilian population of Kabul, as experienced by Laila and Mariam. During this civil war, at the end of which the Hazara faction was defeated, the government forces massacred an estimated seven hundred Hazaran people in the Afshar district of Kabul, soldiers and civilians alike. This Hazara resistance was further weakened by the Taliban and completely defeated by 1995. The status of the Hazara and their enforced servitude and lack of education and political opportunities is apparent in *The Kite Runner*'s characters Hassan and Ali. Assef repeatedly refers to Hassan as Amir's Hazara. Assef's Pashtun-oriented nationalist attitude and hate for Hassan as a Hazaran is made directly analogous to Hitler's anti-Semitic nationalism when he first extols the virtues of Hitler (40) and later gives a biography of Hitler to Amir as a birthday present (97). As a Talib leader, Assef speaks of his desire to remove

On August 8, 1998, the Taliban took control of Mazar-i-Sharif, giving them control of all major cities in Afghanistan. Human Rights Watch reported that hundreds of civilians were "indiscriminately attacked" in the first few hours of fighting by the Taliban and perhaps also by retreating United Front forces. During the days that followed, the Taliban systematically went house to house to round up and execute men and boys from Tajik, Uzbek, and, in particular, Hazara ethnic groups. (See "Afghanistan: The Massacre at Mazar-i-Sharif," Human Rights Watch.)

the Hazara completely from Afghanistan (284). This is further illustrated by Hassan's murder at the hands of the Taliban soldiers.

Discrimination and harsh, arbitrary punishment go hand in hand in Hosseini's novels providing evidence of the abuse of power by the various Afghan governments. Laila's father is a victim of political whim when the Soviet-backed government removes him from his teaching position. After that he works in a bakery. Later in the novel, Laila and Mariam are escorted back to their home by a police officer after attempting to escape from Rasheed and Kabul. The police officer refuses to let them go, claiming that the law requires that they be returned to their husband. Laila explains to him that he is endangering her and Mariam's lives. The officer replies, "What a man does in his home is his business." When Laila protests further, he remains unpersuaded: "As a matter of policy, we do not interfere with private family matters, *hamshira*" (238). Later, when Mariam is in prison she notes that her cellmates were all in prison for the "common offense of 'running away from home'" (322). The Taliban government is portrayed as opportunistic, violent, and oppressive in both novels, and both *The Kite Runner* and *A Thousand Splendid Suns* portray public executions. In *The Kite Runner,* Amir goes to a soccer game at Ghazi Stadium as he seeks to find those who may know of Sohrab's whereabouts. There he witnesses the public execution of a man and woman during the game's halftime. In *A Thousand Splendid Suns,* Mariam is executed in a similar fashion: publicly in Ghazi Stadium after being condemned without legal advice, without a public hearing, and with no cross-examination or appeal.

Hosseini writes compelling stories through which he questions assumptions and breaks apart stereotypes through the strengths and weaknesses of his characters. He interweaves into the action of his stories the details of history, culture, and daily life in Afghanistan. He challenges his readers to reflect on discrimination and political abuse within their own experience in light of instances of such abuses in a different and unfamiliar country. The attacks of September 11, 2001, and the subsequent wars in both Afghanistan and Iraq are paramount to both novels. Readers bring to Hosseini's novels their knowledge of current events and their emotions, fears, and hopes for the current state of the world. As Hosseini's readers connect with the characters of both novels, they may begin to broaden their perspective of these events to see the repercussions of events beyond the borders of the United States and to see, as Hosseini often reminds his audiences, the interconnectedness of individuals no matter where or how they live.

## DISCUSSION QUESTIONS

- What were your views on the burqa before reading *A Thousand Splendid Suns* and have they changed since that reading?
- How does Assef's stark association with Hitler affect your view of Amir's relationship with Hassan?
- How does this association with Hitler inform your knowledge of the status of the Hazara in Afghanistan?
- Compare the status of Mariam and Hassan. In what ways are they similar and how do they differ?
- What did you know about the history of Afghanistan before reading either of Hosseini's novels? Talk about the complexity of the issues of the various factions and warring parties as presented by Hosseini through the novels. For instance, Laila's mother is opposed to the communists; Laila's father sees some good in them. The Mujahideen are seen as heroes, but soon, they become responsible for the destruction of Kabul.
- Think about the history of women's rights in the United States over the past century. Do you see any parallels in the state of women in Afghanistan as represented by Hosseini in *A Thousand Splendid Suns*?
- Hosseini provides a variety of religious viewpoints throughout the stories of both novels; compare these views with what you know about the variety of Christian or Jewish viewpoints in the United States.
- *A Thousand Splendid Suns* is filled with cultural references to food, clothing, poetry, lifestyles, religion, and history. What one or two areas would you like to know more about and why?
- Hosseini's books focus on the harsh facts of war, domestic abuse, and discrimination, and yet readers find these books to be uplifting and inspiring. Explain your own reaction to these elements and describe your impressions to the overall message of these books.

# 6

# POP CULTURE IN KHALED HOSSEINI'S WORK

Khaled Hosseini's books have topped the *New York Times* Best Sellers lists. As of January 18, 2009, *The Kite Runner* was into its sixty-ninth week on the paperback best sellers list. *A Thousand Splendid Suns* was number one in January of 2008 after thirty-two weeks on the hardcover list and, by May 2008, after forty-nine weeks on the list, it was at number fifteen. In mid-January 2009 after coming out in paperback, *A Thousand Splendid Suns* was number two on the *New York Times* paperback best sellers list (*New York Times Book Review* 2009). *The Kite Runner* was awarded the Penguin/Orange Broadband Reader's Prize as the most popular reading group pick in the United Kingdom in 2006, 2007, and 2008. In 2008, *A Thousand Splendid Suns* came in second to *The Kite Runner*. In August 2007, *Library Journal* noted that both of Hosseini's novels were among the most borrowed library books, with *A Thousand Splendid Suns* coming in at number one and *The Kite Runner* coming in at number three. *A Thousand Splendid Suns* was still on the list in June of 2008. As of July 2008, *The Kite Runner* was at number eight on *Publishers Weekly's* best seller list after 197 weeks on the list. With the paperback due out in November 2008, *A Thousand Splendid Suns* was on the *Publishers Weekly* list for forty-eight weeks, with eleven weeks at number one. On January 19, 2009, the paperback was at number ten on *Publishers Weekly's* trade paperback list. In December 2007, Erika Milvy wrote that *The Kite Runner* had sold 8 million copies and had been translated into forty languages. Boyd Tonkin of *The Independent* wrote that by April 2008, "*The Kite Runner* had been published in 138 countries, translated into 42 languages . . . and sold more than 10 million copies."

## Popular but Not Pop

Khaled Hosseini's book *The Kite Runner* has been a phenomenal success, *A Thousand Splendid Suns* has done well for the author and his publisher, and Hosseini fans are passionate about their love for this author's works. Nevertheless, these books do not lend themselves to commercialization, spinoffs, clothing, or gift shop items. Even the film had a limited release and was not by any means a blockbuster. Its total worldwide gross, according to Box Office Mojo, came to $73,193,878 as of its closing date in April 2008.

What is it about these books that has touched off such a torrent of reading and devotion from readers of all ages? When asked this question, Hosseini emphasizes the love story characteristics of both of his novels, and the universal appeal of stories about human connections. Along with the attraction of themes that ring true to a wide variety of readers, *The Kite Runner* is a novel that can be called a page-turner. Readers note that they stayed up all night reading it, or admit that they were never readers until they read this book and then read *The Kite Runner* five times in a row. Add to these two factors the fact that with both of his novels, Hosseini offers to his readers a rare and rich insight into Afghanistan during a time of U.S. military involvement in the country and you may begin to explain the popular and commercial success of these novels. *The Kite Runner* has become its own category of popular culture.

Nauroz, or Farmer's Day, is celebrated according to the Afghan calendar on March 21. It is a celebration of spring and the beginning of the new year. A day of festivities, people dress up in colorful clothes, plant trees, men play Buzkashi (similar to a no-holds-barred polo match with a goat carcass instead of a ball), and children and adults participate in kite-flying competitions. *Haft mewa*, or seven fruits, is a traditional new year's dish made up of walnuts, almonds, pistachios, dried apricots, red and green raisins, and *sanjet* (seeds from the mountain ash).

## Celebrity: Hosseini the Humanitarian

Both *The Kite Runner* and *A Thousand Splendid Suns* deal with issues of war, discrimination, abuse, and good and bad family relationships. Hosseini's official Web site and accompanying blog are good examples of the kind of atmosphere in which Hosseini fans find themselves immersed. Hosseini devotes a significant amount of space in his blog to discussing conditions in Afghanistan. His post of October 11, 2008, is titled "Optimism or Pessimism—Thoughts on Afghanistan's Future." In this entry he spells out the dire conditions in Afghanistan, including increasing death tolls of U.S. soldiers and Afghan civilians, and conditions of increasing poverty, unemployment, and homelessness. He calls for continued U.S. commitment and focus in Afghanistan. In March 2008, he blogs about the National Geographic Exhibition: Afghanistan, Hidden Treasures from the National Museum, Kabul. That same month, he refers to his *Wall Street Journal* op-ed in which he calls for amnesty for the young Afghan journalism student Sayed Parwez Kaambakhsh, who has been sentenced to death for downloading and distributing an article determined by the Afghan courts to be insulting to Islam. In his November 2008 post, Hosseini thanks his fans and in particular his publisher, Riverhead Press, for donating money to fund a new school.

> They donated money on behalf of all the booksellers, librarians, and educators who supported *The Kite Runner* and *A Thousand Splendid Suns*, and built a primary school in Arababshirali, in northern Afghanistan. The school, which will benefit 270 students, will be a sanctuary of hope and happiness for many children.

Toward the bottom of this entry, Hosseini mentions the progress of the production of the film version of *A Thousand Splendid Suns*, but that is as "pop" as his blog gets.

Hosseini has a unique place in American fiction and is perhaps the only author coming out of the Afghan diaspora writing fiction in English. He is immersed in both the culture of the United States and Afghanistan and is fluent in both languages. This, combined with Afghanistan's place in world events, has contributed to Hosseini's celebrity status and to the interest that the media has had in his books. The interviews and publicity have helped to spread word of his novels to a wide reading public. Named Humanitarian of the Year and appointed as Goodwill Envoy to the United Nations Refugee Agency (UNHCR), Hosseini has used his celebrity status to keep his reading public informed about and aware of issues related to the well-being of the country of Afghanistan and its people. Hosseini, with his thoughtful and informed vision, has done more than just draw attention to Afghanistan, he has provided a three-dimensional look at the country that is neither sentimental nor hysterical, that neither condones nor fully rejects the distinctive characteristics of the multiplicity of Afghan culture.

## BEST SELLERS

### Western Interpretations of Afghanistan

It is evident that many readers are thirsting to increase their understanding of Afghanistan. Since the U.S. invasion of Afghanistan and the sudden emphasis on conditions there, especially that of girls and women, publishers have quickly sought to release books that respond to this interest. As of mid-October 2008, *Three Cups of Tea: One Man's Mission to Promote Peace . . . One School at a Time* (2006) by Greg Mortenson and David Oliver Relin was number one on the *New York Times* Paperback Nonfiction Best Sellers list comfortably completing its eighty-eighth week there. This autobiography has generated an illustrated children's book, *Listen to the Wind: The Story of Dr. Greg and Three Cups of Tea* by Greg Mortenson and illustrated by Susan L. Roth (New York: Dial Books for Young Readers, 2009) and a young readers edition, *Three Cups of Tea* by Greg Mortenson and David Oliver Relin, and adapted for young readers by Sarah L. Thomson (New York: Puffin Books/Dial Books for Young Readers, 2009). *Three Cups of Tea* is the story of mountain climber Greg Mortenson and his work with Pakistani and Afghan villagers to build schools.

Travel writer Rory Stewart's *The Places in Between* (2006) was a best seller and chosen as one of the *New York Times* top ten books of 2006. It tells the story of Stewart's walk on foot across Afghanistan just months after the fall of the Taliban. Stewart uses as his guide the fabled Moghul emperor Babur's own account of his travels across the country. Deborah Rodriguez has written up her experiences working for an aid organization and independently as a cosmetologist in Kabul in her popular work *Kabul Beauty School: An American Woman Goes Behind the Veil* (2007). Rodriguez's book was number ten on the *New York Times* list in April of 2007 and its film version is scheduled for release in 2010. *The Bookseller of Kabul* by Åsne Seierstad (2003) is another book that has had wide appeal among U.S. readers and is an international best seller. In October 2005, while *The Kite Runner* was at number two on the *New York Times* Paperback Fiction Best Sellers list for its fifty-fifth week, *Bookseller* was at number eight in its forty-third week on the Nonfiction Paperback Best Seller list. This book by Danish journalist Seierstad looks at Afghanistan through her interpretation of the home life and practices of one Afghan family. These books all look at Afghanistan and its culture through a Western lens. Some of the writers are more sensitive than others in acknowledging the cultural baggage that they bring to their interpretation. In fact, the subject of Seierstad's book wrote his own story as a rebuttal to what he found to be her gross misrepresentation of him and his family. That book, *Once Upon a Time There Was a Bookseller in Kabul* by Shah Muhammad Rais and published by Rais in Kabul (2007), is, unfortunately, not widely available in the United States.

## The Perspective of Afghan Émigrés

Three works by writers with Afghan roots have appeared since the U.S. invasion. Published before Hosseini's *The Kite Runner*, Mir Tamim Ansary documents his sojourn to rediscover the country of his birth and happy childhood. His father remained in Afghanistan after the Soviet invasion, whereas Ansary, his mother, and siblings moved to the United States. As a young adult, Ansary set out to reconnect with his roots. After September 11 he endeavored to present a more balanced view of the country and so he wrote his memoir. His book, *West of Kabul, East of New York: An Afghan American Story* (2002), is a book that will appeal to Hosseini fans. *The Sleeping Buddha: The Story of Afghanistan through the Eyes of One Family* (2007) is Canadian journalist Hamida Ghafour's story of going to Afghanistan on assignment in 2003. This visit was her first return to her native country since leaving as a small child with her family in 1981. Ghafour tells the story of her Afghan heritage along with the history of the country itself. She provides one of the more balanced views of the chadari (or as it is usually referred to, the burqa) and its history and place in Afghan society. She notes, very much as Hosseini does, that the priorities for Afghan women are "safety and finding food to feed their families" (14) and that, without the anonymity provided by the chadari, women are not safe.

Finally, although born in the United States, American teenager Said Hyder Akbar is a first-generation American whose family maintained close ties with important Mujahideen leaders throughout the period of Soviet occupation, ensuing civil war, and Taliban occupation. He details his time in Afghanistan as he accompanies his father who serves with the post-Taliban, post-U.S. invasion government. Akbar's book, *Come Back to Afghanistan: A California Teenager's Story* (2005), began as a radio documentary for the public radio program *This American Life*. Akbar arrives in Afghanistan ready to claim his identity as a citizen of Afghanistan.

## Personal Testimony of Afghan Women

Some discussion, primarily in academic circles, has been critical of the U.S. obsession with the burqa and the reliance on it as a pervasive symbol of women's oppression in Afghanistan. In particular, some scholars have criticized what they see as Western feminists' ethnocentric appropriation of the burqa as the defining feature of Afghan women's oppression. Some would say that Western feminists and Western media are coaching or encouraging Afghan women to use the burqa as a symbol that will be especially riveting or appealing to Western audiences (Whitlock 2005). As is discussed in more detail in chapter 5 ("Today's Issues in Khaled Hosseini's Work"), Hosseini's characters see both good and bad in the burqa. While it is a physically challenging garment to wear and to move about in, both Laila and Mariam find comfort in the anonymity it provides. Mariam, early in her marriage, sees it as a sign of Rasheed's regard for her. The popular obsession with this particular item of clothing can be seen in some of the memoirs and films that have appeared since September 11. This representation of the head-to-toe covering known as a burqa is an essential feature in the marketing and content of some recent memoirs by Afghan women and to a lesser extent Afghan American women since 2001. In fact, the memoirs appearing on the shelves of bookstores and online shops are almost exclusively by women. Hosseini, Ansary, and Akbar are the few Afghan men making their voices heard at the present time.

Nelofer Pazira is a filmmaker and journalist who grew up and lived in Kabul until 1989. Her memoir, *A Bed of Red Flowers: In Search of My Afghanistan* (2005), covers her time growing up in Afghanistan, her family's escape to Pakistan and then Canada, and her return to Afghanistan. She also documents the making of the film *Kandahar*, in which she starred and which is based on her return to Afghanistan to search for a childhood friend. This Iranian-made film makes extensive use of the visual imagery of the burqa, as worn by Pazira as she attempts to fit in and by local women as they walk from place to place.

In *An Afghan Woman's Odyssey* (1996; reissued 2004), Farooka Gauhari, a former teacher at Kabul University, tells the story of her carefree childhood, marriage, and family life before the Communist coup of 1978. Her husband was arrested following the coup and was never seen or

Some terms of common Afghan clothing:

Hijab: Hijab is an Arabic term for body covering. In general, it is a headcover used by women in the Islamic world. Commonly mistaken as merely a veil, the hijab serves a larger purpose in representing a woman's Islamic identity and morality. It can be compared in Christianity to the nun's habit. The complex ways in which this headcover is worn can communicate social status and kinship.

Burqa: The burqa is described in Hosseini's novel as a complete head-to-toe covering worn by Muslim women, by choice, religious custom, at the insistence of a husband, and during certain times, as required by law. During times of political and social modernization, women in Afghanistan were encouraged to refrain from covering their heads, either with a headscarf or with a burqa. Modernization that included more freedom for women to work outside the home or attend school and to go in public without covering has met with resistance and led to rebellion especially outside of the larger cities. Although Hosseini uses the word burqa, *chadhari* is the more common Afghan term for this item of clothing.

Caracul cap: This is a hat made of the wool of the caracul (or karakul) sheep. Hosseini notes that Hamid Karzai, president of Afghanistan, is known for wearing the caracul cap. The hat is peaked and looks something like a cadet's hat or cook's paper cap.

Pakol cap: This is a cap commonly worn in Afghanistan and known outside of Afghanistan as an Afghan hat. It is a round wool cap, with the brim rolled to make an appropriate fit.

Chapan: This is an Uzbek-style coat worn over clothing. It can be made in a variety of colors and is often decorated with elaborate embroidery.

heard from again. Her book documents the plight of her family and her search for her husband. She presents a counterrepresentation of the burqa (or the veil, as she calls it) in her memoir, which was published before the rise of the Taliban and before the burqa had become the iconic symbol of female oppression. Gauhari was a university-educated woman living in Kabul and she taught at Kabul University until her departure from Afghanistan. She describes the social significance of the burqa for Kabul women: "To an outsider, a veil looked like a veil, nothing important to it. But to those of us who wore it there were big differences. Some veils were chic and stylish, with special shorter cap designs. Veils also differed in the fineness of the mesh, the quality of the material, and the way the numerous pleats were set, narrow pleats being considered more stylish than wide ones" (14). In fact, she and her friends "came to find it not so bad. Under cover, our inner childish feelings came out, released from outside social pressures" (14). She considered it to be "a sign of respect, of growing up and womanhood" (15).

The cornucopia of publications by and about Afghan women appearing since September 11 evidences the popular interest in this topic and the rush of publishers to satisfy the reading public. Some of these recent publications include Masuda Sultan's *My War at Home* (2006); Maryan Qudrat Aseel's *Torn Between Two Cultures: An Afghan-American Woman Speaks Out* (2003); Farah Ahmedi's (with Mir Tamim Ansary), *The Story of My Life: An Afghan Girl on the Other Side of the Sky* (2005); Siba Shakib's *Afghanistan, Where God Only Comes to Weep* (2002); *Zoya's Story: An Afghan Woman's Struggle for Freedom* written with John Follain and Rita Cristofari (2002); *My Forbidden Face: Growing Up Under the Taliban: A Young Woman's Story, the Autobiography of Latifa* written with Chékéba Hachemi (2001); and Melody Chavis's *Meena, Heroine of Afghanistan: The Martyr Who Founded RAWA, The Revolutionary Association of the Women of Afghanistan* (2003). Some of these works are described in chapter 9, "What Do I Read Next?"

## THE MOVIES

### Forbidden but Popular

Film is important in both *The Kite Runner* and *A Thousand Splendid Suns*. Although Afghanistan's film industry has been tiny, producing, according to Tom Vick, "forty-odd movies between the early 1950s and the rise of the Taliban in the late 1990s" (245), it has an important place in Afghan popular culture. Hosseini's *The Kite Runner* characters are fans of *The Magnificent Seven*, John Wayne, Steve McQueen, and Clint Eastwood. They spend afternoons at Cinema Park in Kabul. In *A Thousand Splendid Suns*, Mariam's father runs the local cinema in Herat. On her birthday, *Pinocchio* is playing at the cinema and her father leaves a videotape of *Pinocchio* for Mariam, symbolizing his remorse and regret at having abandoned her. Later, Mariam and Laila find comfort, along with many others in Kabul, through watching the movie *The Titanic* (1997). In fact the market, located in the dry riverbed in Kabul is known as Titanic City. The Taliban banned this film along with other forms of visual representation and many forms of entertainment, including kite

Jalil tells Mariam that his cinema is showing *Pinocchio*. Later, even during the Taliban's rule, *The Titanic* became an obsession, at least in Kabul. Mariam and Laila play Titanic games with the children. Although Afghanistan produces little of its own cinema, it is a popular form of entertainment. Videos were sold on the black market and passed along from person to person during the Taliban period.

flying. After the ban, many films were destroyed, but just as the citizens of Kabul sequestered televisions and videotapes, Laila and Mariam secretly own a television set and videos. They bury their television in the backyard and bring it out to watch *The Titanic*.

In fact there was, and perhaps continues to be, a deep attachment for all things *Titanic* in Kabul. In November 2000, *The Guardian* reported, "Titanic fever has gripped Kabul." Despite the fact that the Taliban had banned all movies, television, and music, underground video shops continued to thrive. Bollywood and action films were the usual top sellers, but suddenly *Titanic* was the runaway bestseller. In the dry Kabul riverbed, the bazaar, which came to be known as Titanic City, offered many items, including shoes, perfume, lipstick, and even rice, with the images from *Titanic* incorporated into the packaging ("Taliban: No Subversive Gateaux"). In January 2001, Melbourne's *Herald Sun* reported that the Taliban religious police had arrested and jailed twenty-two barbers for offering Leonardo DiCaprio, or Jack, hairstyles. The hairstyle includes floppy bangs, known as "Titanics," which were forbidden because hair on the forehead interferes with prayer ("Barbers of Kabul Clipped").

In June 2002, after the U.S. invasion and the removal of the Taliban from Kabul, Robyn Dixon reported that Titanic fever was in full gear, with Titanic cakes making their reappearance after having also been banned by the Taliban. Dixon said that even after film and television were banned by the Taliban government, "most people in the Afghan capital watched pirated copies of 'Titanic' at home on their illegal VCRs" (Dixon). Dixon reported seeing posters of Kate and Leo embracing in the windows of shops all over Kabul. She visited one bakery where a four-man team, including a cake engineer, completed a 132-pound cake designed to look like a ship. Besides cakes, said Dixon, "The bazaars are full of Titanic shampoo, Titanic perfumes, Titanic vests, belts, shoes, pants and chewing gum. Souvenir shops sell Titanic mosaics with the ship laid out in lapis lazuli. . . . Young women buy cheap postcards of the

'Titanic' stars, printed in Pakistan" (Dixon). Afghan film director Siddiq Barmak explains why he believes *Titanic* is so popular among Kabul's residents:

> *Titanic* is a great human interest story. People here compare their fate to the story of the Titanic. There's a ship which sails out and the passengers have a common grief which embraces all their lives. And the people on the ship want to save themselves from their misfortune. I think there is a lot in common with the fate of Afghanistan and the Titanic. We're looking for a way to rescue ourselves. (Dixon, A:3)

In 2003, *The Los Angeles Times'* Kim Barker was still able to report the presence of Titanic fever in Kabul. She noted that, in general, the film goers of Kabul prefer Indian- and American-made action films, but that *Titanic* continued to be a favorite, and in fact, she wrote that it is "a way of life" (Barker)—from Leo's bangs to Céline Dion's rendition of "My Heart Will Go On." Barker noted the availability of such products as Titanic Mosquito Killer, Havoc on Titanic Perfume Body Spray, Titanic Making Love Ecstasy Perfume Body Spray, Just Call Me Maxi Titanic Perfume; Titanic brand toothpaste, facial powder, shampoo, and henna; clothing with Titanic images; and large items, from cucumbers to thick-soled shoes, designated as Titanic. Barker quoted Ali Ahmad who told her, "The story is good. It's a real story. That's why people still like it. And the love parts—that's what we like" (Barker). Young Afghan actress Marina Golbahari has said that the only film she saw before starring in Siddiq Barmak's film *Osama* was *Titanic*, explaining that she "liked the sinking scene" (Meo).

## Filming *The Kite Runner*

*The Kite Runner* film appeared in December 2007 after its release was postponed one month to make it possible to remove the two young male stars and their families out of Afghanistan and to another country. The filmmakers had reason to believe that there would be anger among some Afghans because of the rape scene in the film. All involved claim to have had no idea that violence against the children might be a problem. In a 2007 interview with Cynthia McFadden of ABC's *Nightline*, Hosseini points out that his book had been out for several years and he has never received a death threat. Although he had heard some complaints about how he represented the condition of the Hazara in Afghanistan, he has received many more positive responses than complaints from members

---

### *The Kite Runner* Film Details

Director: Marc Forster
Producers: William Horberg, Walter F. Parkes, Rebecca Yeldham, E. Bennett Walsh
Screenwriter: David Benioff
Actors: Khalid Abdalla (Adult Amir), Atoss Leoni (Soraya), Homyoun Ershadi (Baba), Zekiria Ebrahimi (Young Amir), Ahmad Khan Mahmoodzada (Young Hassan), Shaun Toub (Rahim Khan), Nabi Tanha (Ali), Ali Danish Bakhtyari (Sohrab), and Said Taghmaoui (Farid).

The two young male actors, Zekiria Ebrahimi playing Amir and Ahmad Khan Mahmoodzada playing Hassan, both won Best Performance in an International Feature Film—Leading Young Performer from the Young Artist Awards. Mahmoodzada also won the Critics Choice Award for best young actor from the Broadcast Film Critics Association Awards. The soundtrack was nominated for five awards, including an Oscar, and was awarded the Satellite Award for best original score. The film also received the Christopher Award for feature film.

---

of the Afghan community in the United States and abroad. Those involved with making the film have said they had no idea that the children would be endangered by their participation in the film. Forster and Hosseini also point out in the McFadden interview that Kabul is a violent place and people face violence and danger there everyday. It is possible to construe that the boys and their families are better off living elsewhere for the time being, but Forster and Hosseini hold out hope that the boys and their families will be able to return to Afghanistan at a future date.

The film has been received with mixed reviews. Some reviewers have praised the film's beautiful cinematography and the director's careful attention to detail. The cast, which includes two native Afghan children with no previous acting experience, and the British Egyptian actor Khalid Abdalla, who learned Farsi (one of the five languages used in the film) for his role as the adult Amir, has been lauded. David Benioff's screenplay has received approval for its faithfulness to the plot and spirit of the novel. The two young male actors and the score have won international film industry awards. On the other hand, the film has been criticized for its slow pace and overly quiet presentation, sentimentality, and excessive villainy, and for the minor changes that were made to the plot (despite its mostly faithful rendition). Hosseini, who claims to have left the filmmaking to the filmmakers, expresses deep satisfaction with the film. The film was released on digital video in March 2008.

## Made in Afghanistan

Few films have come out of Afghanistan since the fall of the Taliban. *Osama*, directed by Afghan director Siddiq Barmak in 2002, was the first feature film to appear by an Afghan director after the U.S. invasion. It had wide release in the United States and received numerous awards. This film, set during the Taliban era, is a tragic drama about a young girl who is forced by her mother and grandmother to dress as a boy so that she can find work and feed the family. *Kandahar* (2001), another well-received feature film, was directed by Iranian filmmaker Mohsen Makhmalbaf. He also directed the documentary *An Afghan Alphabet* (2005), and his daughter Samira Makhmalbaf directed the film *At Five in the Afternoon* (2003), which was filmed in Afghanistan after the departure of the Taliban.

Western directors have focused on the women of Afghanistan. Liz Mermin's *The Beauty Academy of Kabul* (2006) follows a group of American women, including several Afghan émigrés, who travel to Afghanistan to set up a beauty school. This film depicts the cultural barriers Westerners face rushing into a culture they know little about regardless of good intentions. Beth Murphy's *Beyond Belief* (2006) is a film about two women whose husbands were killed in the attack on the World Trade Center and their mission to raise money for widows in Afghanistan. Robin Benger's *Daughters of Afghanistan* (2004) is a highly politicized film about women in different walks of life in Afghanistan. This documentary is especially noteworthy for the special features included on the digital video, which includes an extensive interview with Nasrine Gross, an Afghan American woman knowledgeable and comfortable with both U.S. and Afghan culture, and interviews with the former and present ministers of women's affairs, Dr. Sima Samar and Habibi Serabi. *Motherland Afghanistan* (2007) is directed by Sedika Mojadidi, an Afghan American filmmaker. Mojadidi travels with her father and mother to Afghanistan. Once there, she follows her father, filming him as he treats female patients at different medical clinics. *Afghan Stories* (2002), directed by Taran Davies and Walied Osman, candidly depicts the lives of a handful of individuals shortly after the U.S. invasion. In Davies's film, men are given a voice as well as women. An outlier in this selection of films is the mainstream feature film, Mike Nichols's *Charlie Wilson's War* (2007). Based on the book

> ### *A Thousand Splendid Suns* Film Details
>
> Expected release: TBA
> Director: Steven Zaillian
> Screenwriter: Steven Zaillian
> Executive Producer: Scott Rudin
> Distributor: Sony Pictures
> Production Company: Scott Rudin Productions
>   Hosseini wrote in his blog, March 31, 2008, that the "matters of casting, location, and language have not been decided." In his November 28, 2008, post he wrote, "A first draft of the script is done and the search is on for a director. When there are more updates, I will post them here."

by George Crile (2003), it tells the story of the Texas congressman Charlie Wilson, who during the early 1980s makes the case for the United States to arm the Afghan Mujahideen in their war against the Soviet Union.

## CONCLUSION

Although Hosseini began work on *The Kite Runner* long before the devastating and world-changing attacks on September 11, 2001, and, thus, was not intentionally part of the resulting rush to portray Afghanistan and its people, his novel has become part of this trend in film and publishing. Hosseini, though, offers one of the few independent Afghan perspectives and, at this time, he is the only Afghan writing in English to use fiction to convey his message. Conscious of his status as an immigrant and as a doctor and novelist, Hosseini is careful to point out his lack of expertise in foreign affairs or nation-building. He has, however, taken advantage of his high profile and continues to keep the condition and needs of Afghanistan, as well as the needs of refugees from other countries, at the center of his message to his many loyal fans. He has used his celebrity status to recommend books that present themes that are similar to those in his novels and that communicate messages consistent with his own message about the importance of human courage and the power of love.

## DISCUSSION QUESTIONS

- Describe what you think of as the appeal of Hosseini's novels. How has he reached such a wide audience around the world?
- What elements of plot and action do *Titanic*, the film, and *The Kite Runner*, the book, share? Why might they both be popular in Afghanistan and in the United States?
- Laila and Mariam go to great lengths to keep their television safe. What place does this piece of equipment have in their lives and why?
- How do you see Hosseini's novels fitting into the books coming out on Afghanistan? In what ways do they stand out as unique?
- How do Hosseini's novels reflect contemporary American popular culture?
- Can you imagine reading these books twenty-five years from now? What about 100 years from now? How might your impression of and reaction to these novels change over time?
- Compare one or both of Hosseini's novels to a novel written in the nineteenth century or the early part of the twentieth century that reflects the political and social situation of its time. For instance, compare Hosseini's novels to Mark Twain's *Huckleberry Finn*, or Charles Dickens's *Hard Times*, or Upton Sinclair's *The Jungle*. Why are these books still read today?
- Talk about the movie *The Kite Runner*. Did you watch it in the movie theater or on video? What were your impressions? How well did it represent your interpretation of the novel? Did any of your thoughts about the plot or characters change after seeing the film?
- What do you imagine will be the difficulties in creating a film adaptation of *A Thousand Splendid Suns*?

# 7

# KHALED HOSSEINI ON THE INTERNET

Searching the name "khaled hosseini" on the Web produces more than two million results, including a *Wikipedia* entry, YouTube videos, radio broadcasts, print and online magazine and journal articles, book review sites, book store sites, and a literature map of what Hosseini readers read (they read everything from Ann Coulter to Rabindranath Tagore). Add the phrase "kite runner" to that search and the results narrow to just over 800,000. Swap out "kite runner" for the phrase "thousand splendid suns" and there are fewer than 600,000 results to sort through. Amidst this flotsam and jetsam on the Web, at least a few solid sites featuring Hosseini and his novels are worth exploring.

## THE OFFICIAL WEB SITE

Appearing high on the lists for "khaled hosseini," "khaled hosseini kite runner," and "khaled hosseini thousand splendid suns" is Hosseini's official publisher-sponsored Web site (http://www.khaledhosseini. com/). This should be the first stop for any reader wanting to know more about the author and his books from the author's point of view. In response to questions from readers, Hosseini has made a series of podcasts, which are linked on the first page of the official site (follow "Listen to Podcasts"). There is also a link to information about the Khaled Hosseini Foundation. Delving more deeply into the official site, there are opportunities to purchase the novels, sign and leave comments at Hosseini's guest book, and read his blog or his latest newsletter. Hosseini takes the opportunity to recommend books and authors to his fan base. He has named *What Is the What*, a memoir-novel about one of the Lost Boys of Sudan by Dave Eggers, as his favorite book of the decade (March 2008 blog posting).

The site is divided into pages that present a brief biography, a contact page, a sign-up page to receive news, and information for the media. The "Books" page includes links to "learn more" about each title. That link takes readers to a selection of reviews, a question and answer page with answers provided by Hosseini, and discussion questions. Perhaps the most valuable and interesting part of this site is Hosseini's blog. As mentioned elsewhere in this book, Hosseini devotes a significant amount of space in his blog to discussing conditions and events in Afghanistan. A newsletter started during the "2nd quarter of 2009" includes Hosseini's recommended books and films as well as news, ideas, and responses to readers' questions.

## News and Review Sites

Further down the list of search results there are a variety of sites that provide book reviews, author interviews, and biographical or related information about Hosseini.

### Academy of Achievement

The Academy of Achievement (http://www.achievement.org/autodoc/page/hos0pro-1) has prepared a nice site to recognize Khaled Hosseini. He was inducted into the academy as a "storytelling phenomenon" in 2008. This site was last updated in September 2008 and features a more extensive biography than that available at the official Web site, an interview, a profile of Hosseini's novels, and a photo gallery.

### New York Times

The *New York Times* has a wonderful feature that creates an archive of selected articles on popular topics. It can be searched by a name or topic directly at the *New York Times* Web site (http://nytimes.com) or readers can go directly to the Hosseini archive (http://topics.nytimes.com/top/reference/timestopics/people/h/khaled_hosseini/index.html). The archive includes articles and reviews from the *New York Times* and the "editor's pick" of sites on the Web. *New York Times* articles cover both novels, as well as *The Kite Runner* film and its controversy. Most articles are fully available, but if not, readers are provided with the title, date, lead paragraph, and link to the full article, which is available for a fee or through local public or academic library collections. Outside resources include National Public Radio broadcasts and articles from other media sources such as *Time* magazine and *Salon*. All of these articles are linked for direct online access.

## Time

*Time* magazine includes a link to its 2008 one hundred most influential people (http://www.time.com/time/specials/2007/article/0,28804,1733748_1733752_1735971,00.html). Khaled Hosseini is No. 66 in this list and former First Lady Laura Bush has written the article on him. Former First Lady Bush commended Hosseini not only for his success as a published author but also for changing the world with his work. In particular, she emphasized, he has given a face to the women "under the burqas" and given his readers the means to "look beyond the post-9/11 stereotypes" of Afghanistan. In addition she believed his novels have universal appeal through their complex presentation of human nature. She wrote, "In more than 40 languages, readers everywhere can recognize the best and worst in humanity in his characters—often in the same person."

## Word Press

The Word Press blog (http://wordpress.com/tag/khaled-hosseini/) takes readers to a list of personal blog entries on Hosseini found throughout the Word Press site. Readers provide a wide range of comments from the trivial to the thoughtful, both positive and negative.

## Fantastic Fiction

Fantastic Fiction provides "bibliographies for over 15,000 authors" (http://www.fantasticfiction.co.uk/h/khaled-hosseini/) and makes available basic information about the featured author. Fantastic Fiction has the unique feature of listing books recommended by their authors along with a brief justification. This site is updated on a regular basis. Hosseini's recommendations reflect themes from his own works: war, the human spirit, rising above adversity. He recommends books that suit his taste for a good story. He recommends Anthony Flacco's *Tiny Dancer: The Incredible True Story of a Young Burn Survivor's Journey from Afghanistan* (2005), Erika Mailman's *Witch's Trinity* (2007), Dinaw Mingestu's *Children of the Revolution* (2007), Abolqasem Ferdowsi's *Rostam: Tales of Love and War from Persia's Book of Kings* (2007),

Steven Galloway's *Cellist of Sarajevo* (2008), a collection of stories by debut writer Sana Krasikov, *One More Year* (2008), and Nafisi Haji's *The Writing on My Forehead* (2009).

## ReviewsofBooks.com

ReviewsofBooks.com (http://www.reviewsofbooks.com/kite_runner/; http://www.reviewsofbooks.com/thousand_splendid_suns/) links to freely available reviews of substance. As of January 2009, the site listed eight reviews for *The Kite Runner* and ten for *A Thousand Splendid Suns*. Most of the reviews are from newspapers. ReviewsofBooks.com also provides a summary of the novel reviewed.

## Barnes & Noble

Hosseini's page on Barnes & Noble: Meet the Writers (http://www.barnesandnoble.com/writers/writerdetails.asp?cid=1145572) includes a brief biography, fun facts or trivia, and, most interesting, a list of his top ten favorite novels and favorite films and his 2004 summer reading list. Each recommendation includes a brief reason as to why Hosseini has chosen it. Unlike the list at Fantastic Fiction, all of which are contemporary publications, the books at the Barnes & Noble site are "all time favorites." Hosseini's list includes the well-known classics *Animal Farm* by George Orwell, *Frankenstein* by Mary Shelley, *The Grapes of Wrath* by John Steinbeck, and *The Rubaiyat of Omar Khayyam*. More contemporary works include *The God of Small Things* (1997) by Arundhati Roy, *The Life of Pi* (2001) by Yann Martel, *I Know This Much Is True* (1998) by Wally Lamb, which Hosseini notes explores themes of "[t]roubled love between brothers, regret, overpowering fathers, and the human need for redemption and freedom from the burden of one's own past," themes that are also central to *The Kite Runner*. His favorite films include *The Good the Bad and the Ugly, The Magnificent Seven, Fargo, Lawrence of Arabia, Godfather I and II,* and *Pulp Fiction*. Hosseini is a reader as well as a writer and his long list of 2004 summer reading included thrillers, history, and literary fiction by, among other authors, Wally Lamb, Ha Jin, Mir Tamim Ansary, Jhumpa Lahiri, Stephen King, John Irving, and Z. Z. Packer.

## FAN SITES

Beyond the official Web site where it is possible to leave comments and questions for Hosseini, both MySpace and Facebook have fan sites.

## MySpace

MySpace.com has an extensive list of sites. If readers search "kite runner fan site" they get one hundred pages or more than seventy-five thousand possibilities ranging from video sites to a fan site for the lead actor from *The Kite Runner* film, Khalid Abdalla, to a site for Refugee International, and the usual spoofs and homegrown videos. At the top of the list are two sites for *The Kite Runner* fans that may warrant a visit. The Latino companion to this popular networking site features a fan site for *The Kite Runner*, http://latino.myspace.com/kiterunnerfansite, which includes some Spanish language information and excerpts (primarily in English) from reviews, a summary of the book and film, and some video.

The U.S. MySpace.com site features the "The Official MySpace Kite Runner Fan Site" (http://profile.myspace.com/index.cfm?fuseaction=user. viewprofile&friendid=221979161), which includes, among other things, videos, a blog, and a fan space.

As of January 2009, there appeared to be no fan sites specifically for Khaled Hosseini or *A Thousand Splendid Suns* on MySpace.com.

## Facebook

A search of Facebook, http://www.facebook.com, brings up three pages of Hosseini fan clubs. Facebook started out exclusively as a college site, but has since expanded to allow anyone to join. Because of its more selective origins, it is a uniform and orderly, consistent, and easy-to-navigate site. There is a standard appearance and arrangement for just about every site on Facebook, so readers do not have the garish colors, the slow-to-load videos, and flashing gimmickry that are at MySpace. There are 800 (and increasing) members of the "Khaled Hosseini Fan Club," and the site offers some links to news stories and a discussion board. Another "Hosseini Fan Club" has 27 members, one called "Mr. Khaled Hosseini" has more than four hundred members, and another has over 8,000. Searching by the names of the novels will also bring up fan groups. Each of these groups allows readers to join and share comments with other fans. MySpace and Facebook are both social networking sites. To make the most of these sites, registration is necessary. Registration is free as is signing on to any fan group. Although younger Internet users frequent these sites, adults also use these sites and make use of the networking features offered.

### THE KITE RUNNER FILM OFFICIAL SITE

The official film site for *The Kite Runner* (http://www.kiterunnermovie. com/) provides information about the movie. It includes links for several "chapters" in the movie, although these are image-intensive pages that have more of an aesthetic appeal than substance. A page entitled "Fly Your Kite: Be Good Again" invites the viewer to reconcile or reconnect with someone from the past. When viewers click on one of the kites flying around the page, they see a message that someone has written to someone else. Readers can create their own kite messages by writing a message and include their e-mail address and the e-mail address of the person to whom they are sending the message. Messages are in multiple languages. Other pages at the site provide video segments of the film, the original trailer, a "behind the scenes" view of the film, a place to download wallpapers and icons, a link to a club with a group blog, and a link to "other groups." Most of what is on the club site is no longer valid and was intended to create interest in the film.

## PODCASTS AND VIDEOS

Podcasts, videos, and interview transcripts are widely available on the Web for those with ample Internet access and a certain amount of patience for downloading.

### FLP Podcast

The Free Library of Philadelphia offers podcasts to their author events. On May 24, 2007, Khaled Hosseini was the guest author at the Free Library. The podcast for his presentation is available at http://libwww. freelibrary.org/podcast/index.cfm?podcastID=15. Podcasts for many interesting and well-known authors are available at this site. Readers can subscribe through iTunes at no charge.

### Learn Out Loud

Learn Out Loud (http://www.learnoutloud.com/Results/Author/Khaled-Hosseini/7029) provides access to free and fee-based audio resources. A search of Khaled Hosseini brings up opportunities to purchase audio versions of his novels and two free resources. These resources include a free podcast of "Understanding Afghanistan" (Sunday, September 26, 2004), which is a 54-minute presentation described as "a look into the sociopolitical climate in Afghanistan and the Afghan community in Northern California. See Afghanistan through the eyes of a native, and hear the stories that come from this ancient culture." This event was recorded live at Grace Cathedral in San Francisco. The second podcast features a 50-minute interview of Hosseini with Susanne Pari, Iranian-American author, presented by FORA.tv.

## Podcast from the Library of Congress

Hosseini discusses his childhood and *The Kite Runner* on a podcast from the Library of Congress (http://www.loc.gov/bookfest/2006/pod/hosseini pod.html).

## Borders Media Book Cub

Borders Media Book Club includes a 50-minute-plus video of a book club session with Hosseini (http://www.bordersmedia.com/bookclub/ hosseini). Book club members discuss the book with Hosseini, and he answers their questions. The entire video recording can be downloaded or watched chapter by chapter. There are eleven chapters in all. In this podcast, author and participants discuss both novels. Hosseini provides background, shares information about his family and his childhood, and elaborates on his view of the current and future state of Afghanistan.

In all of his interviews and presentations, Hosseini presents himself consistently. He is frequently asked about whether or not his first novel is autobiographical. To this question, he responds that the Kabul he writes about is the Kabul of his childhood memories, but he and Amir are not the same person. Similarly, he is asked about his childhood in Afghanistan, and he elaborates to a greater or lesser extent on this, but will often tell the story of teaching his family's Hazara cook how to read and his slow realization that some people were constrained to certain roles because of conditions beyond their control. He talks about his view of conditions in Afghanistan, always noting that his point of view is personal and that he is not speaking as an authority. He talks about his experience of beginning high school in Northern California with no understanding of English. He shares his literary influences, his writing practices, and the origins of his novels. He discusses his recent trips back to Afghanistan and describes his work with the United Nations. Hosseini focuses on the human aspects of his novels and, connected to this, encourages readers to look at the people and conditions of Afghanistan from a human and humanitarian perspective. He never deviates from his claim that he writes old-fashioned stories about love and relationships, and that this is the secret to his novels' broad appeal. Afghanistan and its tragic past, however, are always at the center of all that Hosseini talks about. It is clear that he seeks to use whatever means he has to make sure that people are aware of the continuing crisis there and, in this way, as well as through his work with the United Nations, Hosseini strives to aid his native country in its recovery process.

Finally, Hosseini often devotes time to talking about the condition of women in Afghanistan, which he has so graphically portrayed in *A*

*Thousand Splendid Suns.* Hosseini is quick to dispel notions that "all" Afghan men are Rasheeds or Taliban. He also points to the basic needs that many Afghan women have and that these needs—including health care, food, shelter, and safety for them and for their children—far outweigh any detrimental effects of the pervasive and strict social conventions under which Afghan women conduct their lives.

## Learning More about Afghanistan

Several Web sites provide readers with opportunities to learn more about Afghanistan.

## Kabulpress.org

This newsletter out of Afghanistan (http://kabulpress.org/my/spip.php?rubrique60) condemns censorship and has a prominent connection to Afghan PEN and Raha PEN. This site has stories printed in both English and Dari. Raha PEN is an association for independent writers from all parts of the globe. It supports the freedom to speak, read, and write in all formats and genres and about all creative and theoretical subjects without censorship (see http://rahapen.org). Afghan PEN was founded in Stockholm in 1997 as a means to organize and publish writers from Afghanistan without faction and under a common belief in the importance of the written word (see http://www.farda.org/english/index.html). Both PEN associations derive from International PEN, founded in 1921 as an international literary and human rights organization. It has consultative status at UNESCO and the United Nations and its published goal is to "engage with, and empower, societies and communities across cultures and languages, through reading and writing" (see http://www.internationalpen.org.uk/go/home).

## Afghana! Afghan Web Directory

The Afghana! Afghan Web Directory (http://www.afghana.com/) provides links to everything from postconflict reforms and the Soviet invasion, to flags, entertainment, photographs, and a live Web cam. The site features maps, links to chat rooms, and much more.

## Afghanan.net

Afghanan.net (http://www.afghanan.net/index.php) provides news, history, biography, cultural information, a networking site for the Afghan community, and entertainment.

## Afghanistan's Web Site

The Afghanistan's Web site (http://www.afghanistans.com/) provides encyclopedia style information about Afghanistan.

## Afghan News Network and Afghan Online Press

The Afghan News Network (http://www.afghannews.net/) and Afghan Online Press (http://www.aopnews.com/) both link to a variety of news sources and are updated multiple times a day. Afghan Online Press links to news in Pashto and Dari as well as in English.

## The Culture Orientation Project—Afghans: Their History and Culture

The Culture Orientation Project (http://www.cal.org/CO/afghan/index.html) provides an online booklet titled "Afghans: Their History and Culture" that looks at Afghan culture from the perspective of language, family, history, religion, and society. The booklet features chapters on festivities and food, cultural challenges, and music and literature. A final chapter offers a bibliography.

## This Afghan American Life

This Afghan American Life (http://www.thisafghanamericanlife.com/SnapShots/Home.html) is the home of the project founded by writer Mir Tamim Ansary. The project

> aim[s] to explore the Afghan American cultural identity in Diaspora . . . by supporting and promoting Afghan American writers, collecting oral history, and conducting other projects to help make the Afghan-American experience—and the Afghan experience as a whole—visible to the world.

## Hazara.net

Hazara.net (http://www.hazara.net/hazara/hazara.html) provides information about the Hazara from a variety of sources. Separate pages focus on the atrocities committed against the Hazara by the Taliban as well as Taliban-enforced restrictions on women.

## Afghan Cinema

Afghanland.com (http://www.afghanland.com/entertainment/movies.html) provides information about Afghan actors and films produced from 1958 through 1999.

Afghancinema.com (http://www.afghancinema.com/history.html) provides information for films produced from 1968 through 2006.

"Cinema of Afghanistan" on *Wikipedia* (http://en.wikipedia.org/wiki/Cinema_of_Afghanistan) focuses on Afghan film in the twenty-first century and provides links to other articles on actors and directors.

A 2004 online article by Soutik Biswas, "Women Struggle in Afghan Cinema," focuses on the career of Marina Golbahari who starred in the film *Osama* when she was fourteen (http://news.bbc.co.uk/2/hi/south_asia/3995451.stm).

Jasmin Mehovic's 2004 article "Challenges and Promises of Afghan Cinema" for the South Asia Research Institute for Policy and Development (SARID) provides online access to a collection of news, reports, analyses, and reviews (http://www.sarid.net/sarid-archives/04/0404-afghan-cinema.htm).

## DISCUSSION QUESTIONS

- What are the benefits of joining a club or visiting a fan blog?
- In what ways will biographic information about Hosseini add to your enjoyment or understanding of his novels?
- Web resources give you the opportunity to compare Hosseini's point of view with other writers and sources of news and information. Has this enriched, or can you imagine that this will enrich, your understanding of Afghanistan's very different culture?
- We have access to a wealth of news reports and commentary derived from interviews with Hosseini and from his presentations on his novels because of the Web. Reading these documents helps to place *The Kite Runner* and *A Thousand Splendid Suns* into a real-life historical and present-day context of war and fear of terror attacks. If your great-great-grandchild were reading these novels, which elements might they find interesting? Would the setting be of particular interest? Would the conditions of the women seem exaggerated? Would you say that the friendships, the child-parent relationships, and the love stories within the plots allow the novels to transcend the restraints of our present associations of time and place?

# 8

# KHALED HOSSEINI AND THE MEDIA

## BOOK REVIEWS

The popularity of *The Kite Runner* has been phenomenal and, based on the passion readers have for the book, on a par with the popularity of *Harry Potter*. Hosseini's first novel has a devoted fan base of readers of all kinds. Teens, adults, teachers, casual readers, serious readers, and nonreaders have all been attracted to this novel. *A Thousand Splendid Suns* has also done well, but may not have had the same impact had it not been written by the author of *The Kite Runner*. As mentioned elsewhere in this book, these novels present difficult issues and topics set within harsh conditions, and so they cannot have the same kind of commercial impact that goes along with a publishing phenomenon such as the *Harry Potter* books, but nonetheless, it is rare to run into someone who has not at least heard of *The Kite Runner*.

Hosseini's reception by the media has been overwhelmingly favorable. Hosseini is very much in the public eye, but he does not appear to seek out celebrity, and has used the celebrity that he has gained to further the cause of Afghanistan. Opinion on Hosseini's books is not unanimous, although serious critics are few. One writer called Hosseini's books "little more than exotic pot boilers" (Adams), another critic has pointed out Hosseini's excessive reliance on coincidence and his use of simplistic parallels (Steyn), and still another critic points out Hosseini's "taste for melodramatic plotlines; sharply drawn, black-and-white characters; and elemental boldfaced emotions" (Kakutani). But even the harsher critics find something redeeming in Hosseini's novels. Michiko Kakutani who criticizes Hosseini's plots, comparing them to soap operas, finds reason to read Hosseini in the details Hosseini provides about life in Afghanistan. She concludes her *New York Times* review with, "In the end it is these glimpses of daily life in Afghanistan—a country known to most Americans only through news accounts of war and terrorism—that make this novel [*A Thousand Splendid Suns*], like 'The Kite Runner,' so stirring, and that distract attention from its myriad flaws" (Kakutani). Ian McGillis goes even further, suggesting that the melodrama and simplistic storytelling, or the "guileless storytelling manner," is appropriate, even essential for Hosseini's novels. McGillis writes,

> Melodramatic? In any other context, yes, but here such charges are easily countered by the non-fiction accounts of Afghani [*sic*] women themselves, whose world really was one where the line between right and wrong was clearly drawn. Similarly, complaints that the narrative is ploddingly linear simply get trampled in the momentum of the story and the need for its being told. This, one comes to see, is the key to Hosseini's commercial appeal: he has the common touch. Armed with that gift, he is able, without downplaying or cheapening the horrors his characters suffer, to infuse their lives with the possibility of redemption. (McGillis)

Edward Hower similarly criticizes on the one hand, but praises on the other when he writes, "When Amir meets his old nemesis . . . the book descends into some plot twists better suited to a folk tale than a modern novel. But in the end we're won over by Amir's compassion and his determination to atone for his youthful cowardice" (Hower). He concludes his review explaining what he finds to be the compelling nature of Hosseini's novel: "In 'The Kite Runner,' Khaled Hosseini gives us a vivid and engaging story that reminds us how long his people have been struggling to triumph over the forces of violence—forces that continue to threaten them even today" (Hower). In a more colloquial style, Karen Sandstrom comes to the same conclusion as Hower:

> Despite a narrative misstep or two, *The Kite Runner* really is a hit [ . . . ] the kind of novel that will get book-club members yakking. Better yet, its engrossing human tale might inspire American readers to think about a culture that has become important faster to us than it has become familiar. (Sandstrom)

These are just a few examples from the hundreds of reviews of both *The Kite Runner* and *A Thousand Splendid Suns,* which can be easily retrieved from online newspapers and through databases such as *Lexis-Nexis Academic* or *Academic Search Premier* (to name just two of a number of database possibilities). Most reviewers note the value of Hosseini's more detailed and nuanced presentation of Afghanistan, its people, and its culture. They also note some of the same structural weaknesses of coincidence and melodrama.

## INTERVIEWS

Interviews with Hosseini are numerous. Using databases that provide indexing or full-text access to magazines and journals, newspapers, and broadcast transcripts, and that are commonly found in public and academic libraries, you can easily identify interviews that provide substantial information about Hosseini.

Interviews with Hosseini each tend to cover similar ground. Hosseini always manifests a great deal of humility. Just as the critics comment on his old-fashioned storytelling, or straightforward plots, Hosseini, over and over again, refers to himself as a storyteller; he reiterates his love of writing. Interestingly, in an interview with Mark Mullen of NBC News, Hosseini provided some insight into why he chose a medical career rather than that of a writer despite his early interest in writing. He told Mullen,

> I became very goal oriented. When you're an immigrant, there's—there's always this fear of—of failure, of ending up on the streets. And I decided early on I was going to go to medical school and become a doctor. And I pursued that. And then in the background of all that was this writing thing, which I was doing, once I picked up the English. (Mullen)

As the years go by and the popularity of Hosseini's books remains high, Hosseini has become increasingly outspoken about issues related to Afghanistan. In 2008, he penned two op-eds, one in February in the *Wall Street Journal* and the other in October in the *Washington Post*. In his February 2008 op-ed, Hosseini pleaded for the release of a journalist imprisoned under threat of execution in Afghanistan. He also covered this subject at his official blog. The imprisoned journalist was arrested for downloading and distributing an article critical of the polygamous marriage practices of many in Afghanistan. In the latter op-ed from

October 2008, Hosseini criticized the heightened and violent attacks on Barack Obama by some of the McCain-Palin rally goers during the 2008 presidential campaign. He called for McCain, Palin, and those associated with their campaign to condemn the derogatory use of presidential candidate Barack Obama's middle name, Hussein. He pointed out the similarity of his own name to Obama's and wonders whether the McCain-Palin campaign might also find him to be a "paraiah." Hosseini began this op-ed by writing, "I prefer to discuss politics through my novels, but I am truly dismayed these days" (Hosseini, "McCain and Palin Are Playing with Fire").

This statement in itself is enlightening to Hosseini's readers. Hosseini usually stresses the love-story aspects of his novels. When he is asked about the more political aspects of his novels, for instance, whether his critique of Afghanistan is too harsh and whether his representation of social discrimination based on religious affiliation or ethnic heritage has angered his fellow Afghans, Hosseini consistently answers that it is his view that addressing difficult subjects is an important role of fiction. He told Mir Hekmatullah Sadat in interviews conducted for Sadat's dissertation, "Some . . . have called the book divisive and objected to some of the issues raised in the book, namely racism, discrimination, ethnic inequality etc. Those are sensitive issues in the Afghan world, but they are also important ones and I certainly do not believe they should be taboo" (Sadat, 167). Similarly, he told Farhad Azad in an interview appearing in *Lemar-Aftaab* in 2004 that "Fiction is like a mirror. It reflects what is beautiful and noble in us, but also at time[s] what is less than flattering, things that make us wince and not want to look anymore. Issues like discrimination and persecution, racism, etc. are such things." He went on to suggest that these issues must be confronted for Afghanistan to progress. He pointed specifically to

> the mistreatment of the Hazara people, who were all but banned from the higher appointments of society and forced to play a second-class citizen role. A critical eye toward that era is, I believe, as important as a loving eye, because there are lessons to be learned from our own past. (Azad)

It is because Hosseini raises these difficult issues that he has faced any negative publicity. Interviewers began to ask him more challenging questions in the weeks leading up to the release of the film version of *The Kite Runner*. The media covered the film's controversy, which arose when rumors began to circulate that the lives of the child actors playing Hassan and Amir were being threatened for their part in the film's pivotal rape scene. The two young actors and their families publicly expressed fear and unhappiness over the inclusion of the rape in the film, and claimed that they had not known that the children would be filming this scene. When interviewed on this subject, Hosseini and film director Marc Forster expressed deep regret over the situation, and praised the film company (Paramount) for taking the threat seriously and moving the children and their immediate families out of Afghanistan to safety in a different country. When asked by Neal Conan, host of the NPR program *Talk of the Nation*, about the controversial scene and the situation of the children, Hosseini responded,

> The scene in the film is shot in such [an] impressionistic and subtle way that it's quite suggestive rather than being explicit and graphic. You know, I don't think it dishonors anybody. But, you know, some of the controversy around that scene has kind of overshadowed the message of the film as a whole. And although the scene is pivotal to the plot of the story, the film is not about that scene. The film is—the message of the story is really about tolerance. It's about denouncing hatred and bigotry, and it's really about friendship and forgiveness. (Conan)

Perhaps the harshest criticism of Hosseini came from a fellow Afghan-American author. Luke Burbank, host of the "Bryant Park Project" on National Public Radio, talked to Said Hyder Akbar about the film controversy. Burbank asked Akbar, who is co-author with Susan Burton of *Come Back to Afghanistan* (2005), to comment on the impact the rape scene and the ethnic division that it represents could have on the public in Afghanistan. He asked Akbar whether Hosseini can be blamed for the dangerous position in which the two child actors were placed and, specifically, whether he thought Hosseini was "selling out Afghanistan by writing a book that [depicted] this kind of thing?" Akbar responded, having previously suggested that Hosseini's book was not being read widely in Afghanistan,

> [I]t's difficult to say that he is selling out Afghanistan. I could not say about his intentions. But I know that he has defended himself in the past, saying that I felt like this is what literature is for. I agree with that, but I feel like he is writing for an international audience. He is not really writing for an Afghan audience. And in that sense, it does feel like he is perhaps, in a way, selling the Afghan tragedy to outsiders, I would say. (Burbank)

Akbar and Burbank's challenge to Hosseini's motives is one of the few truly negative comments he has received. Despite the general feeling that Hosseini's books, especially his first, does not meet critical literary fiction standards, most reviewers and interviewers agree with the public that it is a book worth reading for its content. Hosseini appears to agree with the critical assessment of his book, consistently referring to himself as an old-fashioned storyteller. Rather than focusing on the phenomenal amount of positive publicity he has received for his books to glorify himself as a writer, Hosseini turns the attention to Afghanistan, the country and its people, and since 2008 has stepped out of his author role to address significant political issues. Hosseini has received an almost unanimous warm reception from a wide range of writers and journalists from many different countries. In his interviews he, without fail, presents himself with humility and gently prods his audience to keep Afghanistan in their thoughts; to remember that Afghanistan is a country of people, not unlike themselves, who have friendships and lovers, who have dreams, and who seek to care for their families in the best way possible.

## DISCUSSION QUESTIONS

- A significant number of reviewers have commented on the melodramatic nature of Hosseini's novels. Many of these reviewers go on to say that despite this drawback the books are important to read for their content and what the reader can learn from them. How would you weigh these two views of the book? In what ways do you agree or disagree with either assessment?
- Burbank and Akbar suggest that Hosseini has sold out by writing a book that criticizes aspects of Afghan culture but that will likely not be widely read in Afghanistan. Do you agree or disagree with this opinion and what leads you to your conclusion?
- What do you think about the way the media treated the problems that arose for the child actors in the filming of *The Kite Runner*? Were they too gentle with Forster and Hosseini or too harsh?
- Do you feel that the focus on *The Kite Runner* controversy was sensational or were there serious issues to be raised and discussed?
- From reading or listening to interviews with Hosseini, do you feel that you have an idea about what he is like and what is important to him? What are some aspects that you find most striking or interesting?
- If you were interviewing Hosseini or had a chance to meet with him, what unanswered questions would you have to ask him?

# 9

## WHAT DO I READ NEXT?

Hosseini's multifaceted novels appeal to readers for a variety of reasons, whether it is for their epic depiction of Afghanistan, their poignant description of family relationships, their narrative of individuals who develop as they face grave decisions, or for their riveting stories. The suggestions below are just a selection of titles that share one or another of the qualities exhibited by *The Kite Runner* or *A Thousand Splendid Suns*. Some of the titles appearing here have appeared elsewhere in this book, and, conversely, some titles spread throughout the book that may also be interesting to Hosseini's readers do not appear here. A list of suggestions such as this list is naturally colored by the knowledge and reading habits of the compiler. The hope is that readers may rediscover old favorites, be introduced to new authors, and find sources of new knowledge as they choose and read from the following recommendations.

### NOVELS, MEMOIRS, AND THE HISTORY OF AFGHANISTAN

Khaled Hosseini was one of the first writers to present a deep and meaningful view of Afghanistan to American readers. The number of such works published and intended for a general audience, including fiction, but primarily nonfiction, has greatly expanded since that time. Many, many works have been published exploring and examining the status of women in Afghanistan, both predating the Taliban and following the

U.S. invasion. In this segment of further reading, you will find works that provide a range of perspectives and that allow readers to have a deeper understanding of the complicated history of a country that is quite different from that of the United States or most of Europe. Reading a selection of these books will inform readers who may have developed a desire to learn more about Afghanistan, its people, and its culture. Although this is a generous selection of books, it is still only a selection. Most titles are suitable for a general audience.

## Women of Afghanistan

**Ahmedi, Farah, with Mir Tamim Ansary.** *The Story of My Life: An Afghan Girl on the Other Side of the Sky.* **New York: Simon Spotlight Entertainment, 2005.**
This is the true story of a courageous Afghan girl, Farah Ahmedi. A Hazara, Farah was born during the Soviet occupation in the village of Ghazni outside of Kabul. By the time she was going to school, the Soviets had fallen and the Mujahideen were in power. Farah describes her mostly peaceful and happy younger days among a large affectionate family. One day, late for school, she takes a short cut to school and encounters a land mine. She is taken to a local hospital where she is kept alive long enough to be chosen by a German organization for medical treatment. Farah describes her two-year stay in Germany, her recovery and rehabilitation after having her leg amputated, her return to her family and the difficulty of her readjustment to life in an Afghan village, and finally the loss of her father, sister, and then brothers. She and her mother escape to Pakistan and are later selected to move to the United States. This story, intended for young adult readers, portrays, first hand, the extreme culture shock and hardship refugees must somehow overcome when they come to the United States.

**Brodsky, Anne E.** *With All Our Strength: The Revolutionary Association of the Women of Afghanistan.* **New York: Routledge, 2003.**
Brodsky spent time with and interviewed members of the Revolutionary Association of the Women of Afghanistan (RAWA) to chronicle its history and work. Founded in 1977, RAWA is a women-led underground organization fighting for the rights of Afghan women. Among other work, they run schools and orphanages, arrange medical care for women and children, and document fundamentalist activity and atrocities against Afghan women. Their work long predates the coming of the Taliban and continues following the U.S. invasion.

The United Nations Educational, Scientific, and Cultural Organization (UNESCO) estimated the adult literacy rate in Afghanistan in 2004 to be 28 percent of the population. According to the World Bank's *World Development Indicators*, 18 percent of females in Afghanistan completed primary school. In 2007, 12.6 percent of females fifteen and over were considered literate compared with 43.1 percent of males. Compare this with the averages provided by the World Bank for South Asia generally in 2004: males, 71.9 percent; females, 46.4 percent.

**Doubleday, Veronica. *Three Women of Herat*. Austin: University of Texas Press, 1990.**
Written before the Soviet invasion, this book provides an interesting look at three women in Afghanistan. At that time, even before the Taliban institution of restrictive policies toward women, many women stayed at home observing purdah. The three women Doubleday writes about in this book are her friends. They are not a representative cross-section of Afghan women. They are from Herat, and Doubleday notes that Herat has a distinct atmosphere within Afghanistan. Doubleday provides an ethnography of Afghan women written long before the discussion of the condition and status of women was as prominent and politically charged as it is in the early part of the twenty-first century.

**Ellis, Deborah. *Women of the Afghan War*. Westport, CT: Praeger, 2000.**
Ellis, author of *The Breadwinner* trilogy, presents an oral history of Russian women whose sons and husbands served in Afghanistan and Afghan women who are survivors of the ongoing warfare and, at that time, rule of the Taliban. She interviewed women in Russia and Pakistan to present the personal side to the news received by most Western readers.

**Lessing, Doris. *The Wind Blows Away Our Words*. London: Picador, 1987.**
Nobel Prize–winning author Doris Lessing offers a reflective and poetic view of the Mujahideen nearly twenty years before Rall's travelogue (see below) during the time they were fighting the Soviet Union. Lessing is in Afghanistan to find out about an all-woman Mujahideen unit. She details many of the problems we are now aware of in the United States. She describes the hardships of the refugee camps, especially the difficulty of obtaining enough food or any kind of medicine for wounds, the prevalence of illnesses and disease, and the lack of education opportunities for the children. Among other objectives, Lessing and her group are

looking for educated or professional Afghan women to interview. An Afghan man explains how hard it will be to find such a woman because whatever their life was like in Kabul, life in the refugee camp requires veiling, sequestering at home, and leaving the house only with the escort of a male relative.

Logan, Harriet. *Unveiled: Voices of the Women of Afghanistan.* New York: HarperCollins, 2002.

Logan visits Afghanistan in 1997 and then again in 2001. Both times she visits the same women, allowing them to tell their story and, when possible, photographing them. The photographs are beautiful and present a multifaceted view of women in Afghanistan.

Mehta, Sunita, ed. *Women for Afghan Women: Shattering Myths and Claiming the Future.* New York: Palgrave Macmillan, 2002.

This is a collection of essays from a conference of Afghan women scholars and activists held at the Graduate Center for the City University of New York in 2001. The essays presented "trace the history of Afghan women's rights, the rights accorded women under Islam, the abuses perpetrated by the Taliban, and women's priorities in post-Taliban Afghanistan" (x). Contributors are from Afghanistan, Egypt, Great Britain, India, Italy, Uruguay, and the United States. Many of the women have worked in Afghanistan as teachers, aid workers, and organizers. All are feminists.

Pazira, Nelofer. *A Bed of Red Flowers: In Search of Afghanistan.* New York: Free Press, 2005.

Written before the 2001 attacks on New York and the Pentagon, Pazira's book is a memoir of her life with her family under the Soviet occupation from 1978 until their escape to Canada in 1989 when she is sixteen. Pazira describes her rebellious childhood, throwing rocks at Russian tanks and being a member of an armed resistance group. Her father was imprisoned at the time of the 1978 coup, but he was later released. The family decides to leave Afghanistan as her brothers become old enough to be drafted into the army. Pazira returns to Afghanistan to look for her friend Dyana. The movie *Kandahar* is based on this search and Pazira records the making of that film with Iranian director Mohsen Makhmalbaf.

Rodriguez, Deborah. *Kabul Beauty School: An American Woman Goes Behind the Veil.* New York: Random House, 2007.

Deborah Rodriguez shares her experience going to Kabul after the fall of the Taliban to work with a nongovernmental organization (NGO). She finds that her services as a cosmetologist are in demand. She arranges for significant product donations and, on a second trip, joins forces with another organization training Afghan women to become cosmetologists (documented in Liz Mermin's film *The Beauty Academy of Kabul*, 2006) but later sets up her own private shop in Kabul. Her story is slated to appear in a 2010 film adaption.

**Skaine, Rosemarie.** *The Women of Afghanistan Under the Taliban.* **Jefferson, NC: McFarland, 2002.**
This scholarly book includes statistics concerning women's status and education from before and during the Taliban rule, with profiles based on interviews with thirty Afghan refugee women conducted by and translated by RAWA. The women interviewed had either recently fled or fled after the Soviet occupation. The interviews were conducted in March, May, and July of 2000.

**Smith, Mary.** *Before the Taliban: Living with War, Hoping for Peace.* **Aberdour, Scotland: IYNX Publishing, 2001.**
Smith has worked with a small health care NGO in Afghanistan. With this book she seeks to dispel the stereotype of Afghan women as "amorphous shapes shrouded in the burqa" (3). She developed close friendships with women in Mazar-i-Sharif and Hazarajat. These women wanted their stories to be told so that the world would know that not all Afghan women had lost their rights and freedoms. As Smith was writing her book, however, both cities fell to the Taliban. Her book had now become a "history book." It is no longer representative of women's lives in Afghanistan, but it does ensure that the voices of Afghan women will "never be completely silenced" (8).

**Zoya.** *Zoya's Story: An Afghan Woman's Struggle for Freedom.* **Written with John Follain and Rita Cristofari. New York: William Morrow, 2002.**
Zoya lost both of her parents during the civil war that destroyed Kabul following the Soviet occupation. She left Afghanistan for Pakistan with her grandmother. While there, she became involved with RAWA and has traveled back and forth to Afghanistan on missions for that organization. In this memoir, she tells her story from her childhood in Kabul under the Soviets, through her work with RAWA.

## History and Reporting on Current Events

**Akbar, Said Hyder and Susan Burton.** *Come Back to Afghanistan: A California Teenager's Story.* **New York: Bloomsbury, 2005.**
After the fall of the Taliban, Akbar's father goes back to work with the new Afghan government. Born and raised in California, Akbar later

joins his father and keeps an audio journal of his experiences for National Public Radio's *This American Life*. During the time covered by this book, his father becomes governor of Kunar Province. Akbar moves quickly from the life of a fairly typical high school boy to a life complicated through his intimate experience within an Afghanistan in a rocky transition. As a college student, Akbar formed his own NGO, Wadan Afghanistan, which facilitates the building of schools and pipe systems in Kunar Province.

Ansary, Mir Tamim. *West of Kabul, East of New York: An Afghan American Story*. New York: Farrar, Straus and Giroux, 2002.
In hopes of representing Afghan citizens, Ansary sent an e-mail to his friends after the events of September 11, 2001, having heard calls to bomb Afghanistan "back to the stone age." The letter was forwarded from person to person until it had become an Internet phenomenon. You can read a copy of the letter at http://tcotrel.tripod.com/afghanletter.html. Because of the popularity of the letter, Ansary decided to write this book in which he revisits his past, chronicles his travels to reconnect with his Afghan heritage, and recounts his youthful days during the American countercultural movement of the late 1960s.

Ewans, Martin. *Afghanistan: A Short History of the People and Politics*. New York: HarperCollins, 2002.
Ewans presents a concise history of the geography, politics, religion, and culture of Afghanistan from earliest recorded times through 2002.

Gannon, Kathy. *I Is for Infidel: From Holy War to Holy Terror: 18 Years Inside Afghanistan*. New York: Public Affairs, 2005.
Gannon was an Associated Press correspondent in Pakistan and Afghanistan from 1986 until 2005. This book is her account of the Taliban's rise to power, the paths that led to that rise, including the intentional and neglectful acts of countries and agencies outside of Afghanistan that contributed to the particular nature of the Taliban rule.

Gauhari, Farooka. *An Afghan Woman's Odyssey*. Lincoln: University of Nebraska Press, 2004.
From April of 1978 when her husband disappeared during the Communist coup of Afghanistan through December of 1980, Gauhari searched for her husband while at the same time making arrangements to leave the country with her three children and extended family. Gauhari studied and taught at Kabul University, and, at the time she was writing her book, she worked in the department of biology at the University of Nebraska-Omaha. She writes about growing up in Kabul and provides descriptions of the formal courtship process,

the Pashtun code of honor for their women, her impressions of wearing the veil, and the difference between life in Kabul and life in rural Afghanistan.

**Ghafour, Hamida.** *The Sleeping Buddha: The Story of Afghanistan through the Eyes of One Family.* **Toronto: McArthur & Company, 2007.**
Ghafour's family left Afghanistan for Canada in 1981. Ghafour provides a history of the country through the perspective of her family history. She goes back after the U.S. invasion to report on progress and conditions. Like many others, she comes to the conclusion that U.S. policy has failed because of its inability to understand the Afghan culture, its failure to consider the true needs of the people, and its desire to impose a capitalist free market society as though this is the only good option. Interestingly, while in Kabul she meets with Deborah Rodriguez who is the author of *Kabul Beauty School* (see p. 112).

**Rall, Ted.** *To Afghanistan and Back: A Graphic Travelogue.* **New York: Nantier Beall Minoustchine Publishing, Inc., 2002.**
Ted Rall is a journalist and cartoonist. In this book, he writes about his experience going to Afghanistan shortly after the U.S. invasion. He writes that he, his wife, and his agent went to "discover the results of our war upon ordinary Afghans. We never expected to find The Truth, because that's impossible. We did, however, attempt to separate propaganda from reality..." (9). Rall's narrative is represented in straight text and in graphic or comic strip form.

**Shah, Saira.** *The Storyteller's Daughter.* **New York: Knopf, 2003.**
Saira Shah is the daughter of the Afghan-British writer and Sufi leader Idries Shah. Growing up in London, Shah romanticized her Afghan origins and sought to discover the country on her own. She travels to Afghanistan as a journalist during the time of the Soviet occupation. She later returns to Afghanistan to create the documentary *Beneath the Veil*, which explores the plight of women under the Taliban. Her book is written as a journal and, in it, Shah details her experiences in her ancestral homeland beginning in April 2001. Her story is one of danger and hope amidst a seemingly hopeless situation in a country that is war ravaged and steeped in poverty.

**Stewart, Rory.** *The Places in Between.* **Orlando, FL: Harcourt, 2006 (originally published in Great Britain in 2004).**
Rory Stewart follows the path of the Emperor Babur across Afghanistan, relating Babur's story as he passes through the different places on Babur's journey. Stewart experiences danger and hardship along with generosity and friendship on his travels.

**Tortajada, Ana.** *The Silenced Cry: One Woman's Diary of a Journey to Afghanistan.* **New York: St. Martin's Press, 2004.**
Inspired by a lecture given by a member of RAWA, Tortajada, a journalist, travels to Afghanistan in 2000 to see conditions for herself. In her book, she reports on what she sees as the Taliban's genocidal policies against the Hazaras and their brutally restrictive policies for women. Tortajada also reports on the courageous resistance of women helping each other by providing medical treatment and education within their sequestered communities.

**Wahab, Shaista and Barry Youngerman.** *A Brief History of Afghanistan.* **New York: Facts on File, 2007.**
Part of the Facts on File "Brief History of" series, Wahab and Youngerman tell the story of Afghanistan from 3000 B.C. to the present day. This series is intended for students and general readers.

## FICTION AND POETRY

**Ahmad, Aisha and Roger Boase.** *Pashtun Tales: From the Pakistan-Afghan Frontier.* **London: Saqi Books, 2003.**
Ahmad brought together this group of traditional tales, which he collected from a Pashtun storyteller. Ahmad provides background to Pashtun code and beliefs and the place of stories and storytelling within the Afghan and, specifically, the Pashtun culture.

**Aslam, Nadeem.** *The Wasted Vigil.* **New York: Knopf, 2008.**
Aslam weaves the ancient and modern history of Afghanistan into his tale of life under the Soviet occupation and the Taliban. The characters in this novel are from Afghanistan, England, Russia, and the United States.

**Ellis, Deborah.** *The Breadwinner Trilogy.* **Oxford: Oxford University Press, 2006 (available as a collection).**
*The Breadwinner.* **Toronto: Douglas & McIntyre, 2001.**
*Parvana's Journey.* **Toronto: Douglas & McIntyre, 2001.**
*Mud City.* **Toronto: Groundwood Books, 2003. (Juvenile/Teen Literature)**
In the *Breadwinner* and *Parvana's Journey,* Ellis introduces the reader to life in Afghanistan under the Taliban. Parvana's father is arrested and she must dress like a boy so that she can go to the market and find ways to earn money. She makes friends with a former schoolmate, Shauzia, who is also dressed as a boy in her attempt to earn money for her family. The family is separated in the chaos of war and in book two Parvana

seeks to find the surviving members of her family. She and Shauzia have agreed to meet in Paris in twenty years. In *Mud City*, Ellis tells the story of Shauzia. Like Parvana, she is a resourceful and fearless girl fighting for some kind of meaningful life under conditions in which others have understandably given up. Her hope is to make her way to the ocean (Afghanistan is landlocked) and then to travel to France to live in a field of lavender.

Ellis concludes her novels with information about Afghanistan, the wars, and the conditions there, especially for women and children. The royalties from the sales of *Parvana's Journey* go to Women for Women, an organization that helps women in Afghanistan. Ellis is donating the royalties from *Mud City* to Street Kids International, a nonprofit organization that works with children around the world who are living on the streets.

**Khadra, Yasmina. *Swallows of Kabul*. New York: Nan A. Talese, 2004.**
Khadra is the alias of an Algerian army officer who writes in French. This novel is set under the Taliban and in Kabul, as the title suggests. Khadra's novel is a tale of unrelenting misery. Its unusual plot features two couples. The first couple has lived a life of relative privilege; the husband is from a successful family of shopkeepers and his wife is an educated teacher. When the wife accidentally kills her husband during an argument, she is taken to the women's prison. There the husband of the second couple sees her when she removes her burqa. Having not seen a woman's face other than that of his continuously ailing wife in years, he sees the prisoner as a vision and sets about devising a way to prevent her execution.

**Majrouh, Sayd Bahodine. *Songs of Love and War: Afghan Women's Poetry*. Translated from the Pashtun into French. Adapted and introduced by André Velter and the author. Translated from the French by Marjolijn De Jager, New York: Other Press, 2003.**
Afghan poet Majrouh tells the story of Pashtun women from Afghanistan and the Afghan refugee camps in Pakistan through their *landays*, two-line verses of nine and thirteen syllables. The verses represent experiences of love, war, passion, and desolation. Velter provides a brief biography of Majrouh, with whom he worked to publish his poetic works in French under the title *Ego Monster* (1989–1991). Majrouh was assassinated in Peshawar in 1988.

**Marciano, Francesca. *The End of Manners*. New York: Pantheon Books, 2008.**
Maria Galante and Imo Glass are female journalists, Maria a photographer and Imo a writer. Maria reluctantly agrees to accompany Imo to

Afghanistan to photograph women who have attempted suicide rather than marry the older men chosen for them by their families. Imo is experienced but insensitive to the subtleties and restrictions for women within the Afghan culture. Maria is inexperienced but more open to the sensibilities of the people with whom she is working.

**Shah, Idries.** *Kara Kush: A Novel of Afghanistan.* **New York: Stein and Day, 1986.**
Shah, the leader of the Sufis and a scholar in the field, wrote this, his only novel, as recognition of the ongoing fight against the Soviet occupation in the land of his ancestry. It is written as an adventure novel with intrigue and action.

**Staples, Suzanne Fisher.** *Under the Persimmon Tree.* **New York: Farrar, Straus and Giroux, 2005.**
This is the story of Najmah, a shepherd girl from Kundunz, and Nusrat, an American woman married to an Afghan doctor and living in Peshawar, Pakistan, near the Afghan refugee camps. The Taliban have taken Najmah's father and brother away and her mother and small brother are killed in a shelling attack. She travels to Pakistan with neighbors and ends up leaving them only to find her way to Nusrat's small school that she operates for refugee children. Nusrat's husband has been away in Mazar-i-Sharif to work in a clinic and she has stayed in Peshawar to continue to work with refugee children. She takes Najmah under her wing. Later, Najmah's brother appears and together they decide to return to their land in Kunduz to try to maintain the family farm. Nusrat goes to Mazar-i-Sharif to see what she can find out about her husband.

**Yermakov, Oleg.** *Afghan Tales: Stories from Russia's Vietnam.* **Translated by Marc Romano. New York: William Morrow, 1991.**
Yermakov's stories are all in some way about the Soviet occupation of Afghanistan. Beautifully written, they present a seldom-heard voice in the tragic saga of modern-day Afghanistan.

## NOVELS ABOUT FAMILIES, GENDER, DISCRIMINATION, AND IMMIGRATION

In this category, readers will find novels and, in one case, a memoir and collection of essays that explore familial relationships as well as issues of gender, discrimination, and immigration. Many of the suggested titles are well known and considered twentieth-century classics. Some are new contributions to the rich literary tradition established by their critically acclaimed predecessors.

**Cather, Willa.** *My Antonia.* **Lincoln: University of Nebraska Press, 2009.**
Cather intertwines the lives of Bohemian immigrant Antonia and her childhood friend Jim Burden in this novel. Told mostly through the perspective of Jim, *My Antonia* represents the epitome of pioneer life with its sense of freedom, reinvention, struggles, and disappointments.

**Lamming, George.** *The Emigrants.* **Ann Arbor: University of Michigan Press, 1994.**
Lamming tells the story of a group of West Indians who immigrate to Great Britain. They leave their native countries in search of education opportunities but find that "the mother country" is not as welcoming or as easy to settle into as they had expected. The novel follows the stories of a range of characters who respond to their new surroundings in a variety of ways, but all of whom experience marginalization and isolation within their adopted country. This book was first published in the United States in 1955 by McGraw Hill.

**Lee, Harper.** *To Kill a Mockingbird.* **New York: HarperCollins, 2006.**
This much-loved novel tells the story of strong family ties, and learning, through a father's example, to see people for who they really are and not through the lens of ignorance and prejudice. Set in the Deep South that is defined by its racism, Lee's novel tells the story of Scout's coming of age, as her father takes on the defense of a black man who has been charged with rape.

**Némirovsky, Irène.** *Suite Française.* **New York: Alfred A. Knopf, 2006.**
Némirovsky was born into a Jewish family in Russia and immigrated with her family to Paris in the 1920s. She began to record the chaos and disruption of the Nazi occupation of France in what she planned as a five-novel cycle. She had completed manuscripts for two novels and had begun notes for the third when she was arrested by the Nazis and sent to Auschwitz where she was almost immediately sent to the Birkenau death camp. Némirovsky had already achieved popularity as a writer before beginning her five-novel project. Her daughters kept the manuscripts and the first two novels were published together as *Suite Française* nearly seventy years after Némirovsky completed them. Némirovsky writes about events following the Nazi occupation as they were unfolding. She focuses on the details of her characters' daily lives with the war and historical facts providing the backdrop. Rochelle Goldberg Ruthchild writes, "Her remarkable work vividly takes the reader back to the early stages of the last major war in the heartland of Europe.

Her keen observations about the chaos of war, ruling class complicity and cowardice, individual heroism, collaboration, lies and rationalizations, and militarized, random violence unfortunately remain all too timely today" (23).

Rodriguez, Richard. *Hunger of Memory: The Education of Richard Rodriguez.* Boston: David R. Godine, 1982.
Rodriguez grew up in a Spanish-speaking household in California. He began to learn English as he entered school. He writes about the importance of learning English and becoming part of the culture of his parents' adopted country. His immersion into the English-speaking world, however, causes him to feel a growing separation from his family. Rodriguez earned a doctorate in English studying at the University of California–Berkeley and in England. He finds that he questions the validity of his multiple job offers in light of the controversy of affirmative action and he turns them all down. Rodriguez's autobiography was controversial when it first appeared because of his criticism of bilingual education and affirmative action; however, he notes in his prologue that it is the story of his life and thus reflects only his experiences.

Rodriguez, Richard. *Days of Obligation: An Argument with My Mexican Father.* New York: Viking, 1992.
Rodriguez continues to explore issues of ethnicity and immigration in this collection of essays.

Rølvaag, Ole Edvart. *Giants in the Earth: A Saga of the Prairie.* New York: HarperCollins, 1999.
This novel, set at the end of the nineteenth century, presents the story of Per and Beret Hansa, immigrants from Norway to the Dakotas early in that area's settlement by European immigrants. The intense solitude and a treeless open prairie drive Beret close to insanity and the hard work and harsh environment lead to Per's death. *Giants in the Earth* is followed by two more novels, which continue the story of Beret and her children: *Peder Victorious* (1929) and *Their Father's God* (1931).

Saroyan, William. *My Name is Aram.* New York: Dell Publishing, 1991.
This novel, a series of connected stories, is the fictional account of William Saroyan's childhood, the son of Armenian immigrants in rural Fresno, California.

Satrapi, Marjane. *Persepolis I* and *Persepolis II: The Story of a Return.* New York: Pantheon Books, 2003 and 2004.
This autobiographical graphic novel tells of Satrapi's childhood in Iran growing up during the revolution in a family who first protested the

Shah's regime and then the revolutionary regime. Satrapi has a tendency to get into trouble and so her parents send her out of the country. This turns out to be a disastrous step for Satrapi, and she eventually returns to her family in poor physical and mental health. When she regains her strength, she is determined to reject victimhood and attends university to study art. She eventually marries, although it does not lead to a happy ending. Satrapi's novels were adapted into an animated film in 2007 by directors Vincent Paronnaud and Marjane Satrapi.

**Smith, Betty.** *A Tree Grows in Brooklyn.* **New York: HarperCollins, 2008.**
Francie Nolan grows up in the poor neighborhoods of Brooklyn. The tree growing outside her tenement apartment represents the persistence of beauty in a bleak landscape and the possibility of thriving even under harsh conditions. Francie's imagination, love of reading, and determination to thrive under all circumstances are at the center of this novel.

**West, Dorothy.** *The Wedding: A Novel.* **New York: Knopf, 1996.**
West writes about community, family, generational values and change, marriage, race, and discrimination in her novel about tensions within an aristocratic black family and community on Martha's Vineyard in the 1950s.

## Epic Novels

These historical novels depict significant events, in many cases across decades and generations.

**Erdrich, Louise.** *Love Medicine.* **New York: Holt, Rinehart, and Winston, 1984; revised edition, 1993.**
*The Beet Queen.* **New York: Holt, 1986.**
*Tracks.* **New York: Holt, 1988.**
*The Bingo Palace.* **New York: HarperCollins, 1994.**
*Tales of Burning Love.* **New York: HarperCollins, 1996.**
These five novels make up Erdrich's North Dakota cycle of novels. They share an interrelated set of characters from the Chippewa and non–Native American worlds of North Dakota and are set both on and off the reservation. The stories are told from the perspectives of multiple first-person narrators and evoke a world in which cultures and languages mingle in conflicting and enriching ways.

Esterhazy, Peter. *Celestial Harmonies: A Novel*. Translated by Judith Sollosy. New York: Ecco Press, 2004.
Esterhazy is descended from the Esterhazys who were central figures in the Hapsburg empire. The book is divided into two sections, with the first portraying the Esterhazy men from the earliest days of the Hapsburg empire through to its disintegration in the early part of the twentieth century and on to the present. In the second section, Esterhazy tells the story of his own family from the time of the Russian Revolution through to his own generation.

Hegi, Ursula. *The Vision of Emma Blau*. New York: Simon and Schuster, 2000.
This story covers one hundred years of a family's history, beginning with Stefan Blau's escape from his small village in Germany to Manhattan. He begins to work in the restaurant business, and after surviving a tragic fire, he becomes obsessed with fire safety. He builds a fireproof apartment complex as he begins to raise his family. After the loss of two wives, Blau returns to Germany to marry his third wife who raises his two surviving children and brings a third into the world. Emma is Stefan's granddaughter and she absorbs his love for his apartment building in which everyone in the family has grown up. After the death of Stefan and his third wife, however, the apartment building drives the family apart.

Lessing, Doris May. *The Cleft*. New York: HarperCollins, 2007.
Lessing explores relationships between men and women in this mythological history of a community of women known as The Cleft. The women have lived and reproduced successfully without knowledge of men. This all changes when a male child is born.

Lins, Paulo. *City of God*. Translated by Alison Entrekin. New York: Black Cat, 2006.
This novel tells the story of a family in Rio de Janeiro living in the poverty-stricken, drug-infested corner known as City of God. The story is told over two generations and three decades.

Shih Shu-Ching. *City of the Queen: A Novel of Colonial Hong Kong*. Translated from the Chinese by Sylvia Li-Chun Lin and Howard Goldblatt. New York: Columbia University Press, 2005.
This novel traces the evolution of the colonial city of Hong Kong through the life of one woman and her family. Huang is kidnapped as a child and sold into prostitution. Through her ingenuity, she makes her way out of servitude to become a landowner. Her children prosper, but their children's children are seduced by the pleasurable offerings of the

late-twentieth-century city. *City of the Queen* examines colonialism, the colonizers, and the colonized.

**Steinbeck, John. *Grapes of Wrath*. New York: Viking, 1989.**
Originally published in 1939, *Grapes of Wrath* tells the story of a family forced from their home by the dust bowl, their tortuous journey to California, and their continued hardships once they arrive.

**Tademy, Lalita. *Cane River*. New York: Warner Books, 2001.**
***Red River*. New York: Warner Books, 2006.**
Both of these books come out of Tademy's research into her family's history as slaves and slaveholders on the plantations of Louisiana. *Cane River* follows the lives of four generations of women from slavery, through the Civil War, and into Reconstruction and the early twentieth century. *Red River* focuses on the riots that dispossessed the newly freed African Americans in the town of Colfax, Louisiana. Once again, this novel traces the history of a family through its women and across generations.

**Torvik, Solveig. *Nikolai's Fortune*. Seattle: University of Washington Press, 2005.**
Based on the story of her own family and its origins in Finland and Norway, author Torvik writes a multigenerational epic of love, hardship, emigration, and sometimes bitter survival. The younger generations adapt to the new land unable to fully grasp the history of their elders. She divides her novel into three parts, the first from the point of view of the grandmother, the second in the voice of the daughter, and the third narrated in the voice of the granddaughter.

## Novels and Memoirs about Fathers and Sons

**Bower, Kenneth. *Starship and the Canoe*. New York: Holt, Rinehart, and Winston, 1978.**
This is the story of a father, astrophysicist Freeman Dyson, and son George who have different interests but nevertheless have many shared characteristics as well. The senior Dyson is designing a nuclear-powered spaceship, while his son is building a giant seagoing canoe and living in a tree in British Columbia.

**Hijuelos, Oscar. *Mr. Ives' Christmas*. New York: HarperCollins, 1995.**
Mr. Ives's son is murdered in a random robbery and Mr. Ives does not recover. Through a priest, the murderer has sought Mr. Ives's forgiveness. Finally, thirty years later, Mr. Ives is ready to consider the possibility.

**Lamb, Wally.** *I Know This Much Is True.* **New York: Regan Books, 1998.**
Hosseini recommends this novel whose characters deal with issues of mental illness, abuse, and neglect. The lives of twins Thomas and Dominic are chronicled in Lamb's novel. Thomas suffers from schizophrenia and Dominic is recovering from a difficult divorce, trying to help his brother, and investigating their family history, including unearthing the identity of their birth father.

**Obama, Barack.** *Dreams from My Father: A Story of Race and Inheritance.* **New York: Times Books, 1995.**
Obama published his memoir more than a decade before he became a household name and the president of the United States. Obama's story begins as he learns of his father's sudden death in a car accident. Never having had the opportunity to spend much time with his father, Obama decides to explore the origins of both of his parents, his mother from a small town in Kansas, and his father from Kenya. His parents meet in Hawaii where Obama is born. Obama traces his education and career path through to 1995 and reflects on his identity in light of his bicultural heritage.

**Wideman, John.** *Fatheralong: A Meditation on Fathers and Sons, Race and Society.* **New York: Pantheon, 2004.**
Wideman considers his relationship with his father as he reflects on his relationship with his son.

## *Bildungsromane* and Coming-of-Age Narratives and Memoirs

Many novels that are classified as *bildungsromane* might also be considered epic novels because they span years, continents, and decades. Literature, like knowledge, rarely fits into one neat category. These novels are all in some way coming-of-age stories and follow the main character, whether through a first-person narrative or through an omniscient third-person narrative, through a lifetime, revealing the events and experiences that bring that character to a fuller understanding of him- or herself in relation to the world and to those important to them.

**Cheng, Terrence.** *Sons of Heaven.* **New York: William Morrow, 2002.**
Cheng constructs a life for the young man who stood before the tanks in the midst of the Tiananmen Square massacre of 1989. In this novel, the young man goes to the United States for his education and returns to a China he no longer finds hospitable. His disillusionment leads him to join with other dissidents as they occupy the square. The young man's

older brother is a dedicated soldier sent with his platoon to quell the demonstration at Tiananmen Square and then later to find and arrest his younger brother. Cheng also imagines the thoughts and motivations of Deng Xiaoping as he orders the army into Beijing and then experiences the consequences of having issued that order.

**Dickens, Charles. *Barnaby Rudge: A Tale of the Riots of '80*, 1841.**
This lesser known novel by Dickens, with his characteristic intricate plot and complexity of characters, follows the course of the simpleton Barnaby Rudge who floats among the different events and households portrayed in the novel. Set in London at the end of the eighteenth century, the novel evolves around the anti-Catholic Gordon Riots of 1780. Dickens, in his preface, writes,

> It is unnecessary to say, that these shameful tumults [the riots], while they reflect indelible disgrace upon the time in which they occurred, and all who had act or part in them, teach a good lesson. That what we falsely call a religious cry is easily raised by men who have no religion, and who in their daily practice set at nought the commonest principles of right and wrong; that it is begotten of intolerance and persecution; that it is senseless, besotted, inveterate, and unmerciful; all History teaches us.

These words are still valid and also evoke Hosseini's sentiments as represented in his novels.

***The Life and Adventures of Martin Chuzzlewit*, 1844.**
This sprawling novel follows the fate of the young Martin Chuzzlewit, who looks for fame and fortune out from under the wing of his controlling and repressive grandfather. His travels take him to America, where he suffers hardship but returns to England humbled by the crass materialism and shallow hubris he has witnessed while away.

**Green, Hannah. *The Dead of the House*. New York: Doubleday, 1972 and Books & Co., Turtle Point Press, 1996.**
This is a novel based on the family history of the author. Vanessa, the main character, recalls the stories she heard from her paternal grandfather as a child and her own relationships with a complicated and eccentric extended family. The story ends as she and her siblings and cousins begin to deal with the issues of adulthood, the births of the next generation, and the death of their grandfather.

**McEwan, Ian.** *Atonement.* **New York: Vintage, 2002.**
McEwan's novel, one of Hosseini's own recommendations, has many similarities to *The Kite Runner.* He tells the story of the developing writer Briony Tallis over six decades and two world wars. She commits an act for which she feels intense guilt and attempts to make up for it through her actions later in life.

**Rouaud, Jean.** *The Jean Rouaud Trilogy.*
*Fields of Glory.* **New York: Arcade Publishing, 1992.**
*Of Illustrious Men.* **New York: Arcade, 1994.**
*The World More or Less.* **New York: Arcade, 1998.**
These are the first three in a series of five autobiographical novels through which the author portrays his family and his own journey to becoming a writer. The final two novels have not yet been translated into English. Rouaud's rural family has been ravaged by the two world wars. The novels are written from a variety of perspectives: the first novel written from the perspective of his grandfather and the second from that of his father. In the third novel, Rouaud focuses on his own coming of age. In the final two novels, *Pour vos cadeaux* (1998) and *Sur la scène comme au ciel* (1999), Rouaud writes about his mother and his relationship with her.

**See, Lisa.** *Peony in Love: A Novel.* **New York: Random House, 2007.**
This historical novel is set in seventeenth-century China. See follows the development of Peony, a protected child, who nonetheless falls in love when she glimpses a handsome young man through a protective curtain. Much of the story takes place after her death.

**Thomas, Piri.** *Down These Mean Streets.* **New York: Knopf, 1967.**
Thomas is twelve years old in 1941 as he begins his memoir. It is just before the attack on Pearl Harbor. He is a first-generation American, the oldest son in a large Puerto Rican family living in Harlem. His father has lost his job, but with the advent of war, the father finds work in an airplane factory. The family moves to Long Island and, in this predominantly white neighborhood, Thomas begins to become aware of the fact that he is the only child to have inherited his father's African coloring and features. The other children take after their more European featured mother. Thomas's anger continues to grow and divides him from his family. He leaves home to find his own way. Convicted of armed robbery, he spends time in prison, and, while there, begins to educate himself.

# RESOURCES

Abdullah, Farid. "Afghan Cinema Site 'Bod na Bod'" http://www.afghan cinema.com/history.html (accessed June 30, 2009).

Adamec, Ludwig. *Historical Dictionary of Afghanistan.* 3rd ed. Lanham, MD: Scarecrow Press, 2003.

Adams, Lorraine. "Torch Song for Afghanistan." *New York Times*, October 12, 2008, sec. Book Review Desk.

"Afghan Kite History. "planet.kite.matrix (world kite project)." http://subvision. net/sky/planetkite/middle-east/afghanistan/ (accessed August 31, 2008).

"Afghanistan." In *Encyclopedia Britannica.* Encyclopedia Britannica Online, 2008. http://search.eb.com/eb/article-21424 (accessed May 26, 2008).

"Afghanistan: The Massacre at Mazar-i-Sharif." *Human Rights Watch* 10, no. 7 (C) (November 1998). http://www.hrw.org/legacy/reports98/afghan (accessed May 3, 2009).

"Afghanland Movie Review." Afghanland.com. http://www.afghanland.com/ entertainment/movies.html (accessed January 12, 2009).

Ahmadi, Walid. *Modern Persian Literature in Afghanistan: Anomalous Visions of History and Form.* New York: Routledge, 2007.

Ahmedi, Farah, with Mir Tamim Ansary. *The Story of My Life: An Afghan Girl on the Other Side of the Sky.* New York: Simon Spotlight Entertainment, 2005.

Akbar, Said Hyder and Susan Burton. *Come Back to Afghanistan: A California Teenager's Story.* New York: Bloomsbury, 2005.

Ansary, Mir Tamim. *West of Kabul, East of New York: An Afghan American Story.* New York: Farrar, Straus and Giroux, 2002.

Aseel, Maryan Qudrat. *Torn Between Two Cultures: An Afghan-American Woman Speaks Out.* Sterling, VA: Capital Books, 2003.

Ayotte, Kevin J., and Mary E. Husain. "Securing Afghan Women: Neocolonialism, Epistemic Violence, and the Rhetoric of the Veil." *NWSA Journal* 17, no. 3 (2005): 112–133.

Azad, Farhad. "Dialogue with Khaled Hosseini Afghan Magazine." *Lemar-Aftaab, afghanmagazine.com* 3, no. 4 (June 2004). http://www.afghan magazine.com/2004_06/profile/khosseini.shtml (accessed January 20, 2009).

"Barbers of Kabul Clipped." *Herald Sun* (Melbourne, Australia), January 27, 2001, 019.

Barker, Kim. " 'Titanic' Rises as Taliban Sinks." *Los Angeles Times*, April 22, 2003, E8.

Bookbrowse.com and Khaled Hosseini. "Author Interviews: Khaled Hosseini." Bookbrowse.com, 2007. http://www.bookbrowse.com/author_interviews/full/index.cfm?author_number=900 (accessed September 7, 2008).

Box Office Mojo. "The Kite Runner." Box Office Mojo, LLC, 2008. http://www.boxofficemojo.com/movies/?id=KiteRunner.htm (accessed November 6, 2008).

Buckley, Jerome Hamilton. *Season of Youth: The Bildungsroman from Dickens to Golding*. Cambridge, MA: Harvard University Press, 1974.

Burbank, Luke. "Film Roles Lead to Fear in Afghanistan." National Public Radio, "The Bryant Park Project," October 8, 2007 (transcript retrieved from *LexisNexis Academic*).

Burr, Ty. "Returning to Afghanistan, with a Heavy Heart: A Less-than-Novel Take on a Bestseller." *Boston Globe*, December 14, 2007, sec. LIVING ARTS: C1. http://www.boston.com/ae/movies/articles/2007/12/14/returning_to_afghanistan_with_a_heavy_heart/ (accessed January 20, 2009).

Central Intelligence Agency. *2008 World Factbook*. https://www.cia.gov/library/publications/the-world-factbook/index.html (accessed May 4, 2009).

Chavis, Melody. *Meena, Heroine of Afghanistan: The Martyr Who Founded RAWA, the Revolutionary Association of the Women of Afghanistan*. New York: St. Martin's Press, 2003.

Conan, Neal. "Afghanis Face Uncertain Future." National Public Radio, *Talk of the Nation*, November 1, 2007 (transcript retrieved from *LexisNexis Academic*). http://www.npr.org/templates/story/story.php?storyId=15850610 (accessed October 29, 2008).

Conlogue, Ray. "Afghanistan's Next Chapter." *Globe & Mail*, June 12, 2003, R:1.

Coughlin, Kathryn M. *Muslim Cultures Today: A Reference Guide*. Westport, CT: Greenwood Press, 2006.

Cowan, James and Khaled Hosseini. "The Nation We Don't Know." *National Post* 5, no. 211 (2003): PT6.

Crile, George. *Charlie Wilson's War*. Atlantic Monthly Press, 2003.

Davis, Diana. "How Can We Be Koochi?" *Cultural Survival Quarterly* 16, no. 4 (October 1992).

Defoe, Daniel. *Robinson Crusoe.* 1739. New York: Norton, 1975.

Dennis, Matthew. "Afghanistan." In *Encyclopedia of Holidays and Celebrations: A Country-by-Country Guide.* Facts on File Library of World History. New York: Facts on File, 2006

Dixon, Robyn. "Once Unthinkable, Now Unsinkable." *Los Angeles Times,* June 2, 2002, A.

Eggers, Dave. *What Is the What: The Autobiography of Valentino Achak Deng: A Novel.* San Francisco: McSweeneys, 2006.

Ellis, Deborah. *Women of the Afghan War.* Westport, CT: Praeger, 2000.

Emadi, Hafizullah. *Repression, Resistance, and Women in Afghanistan.* Westport, CT: Praeger, 2002.

Embassy of the Islamic Republic of Afghanistan in Italy. http://www.afghanistan embassyitaly.com/home.htm (accessed August 31, 2008).

Ember, Melvin and Carol R. Ember. *Countries and Their Cultures.* New York: Macmillan Reference USA, 2001.

Esposito, John. *Oxford Encyclopedia of the Modern Islamic World.* New York: Oxford University Press, 1995.

Europa Publications Limited. *South Asia: 2008.* 5th ed. Regional Surveys of the World. London: Europa Publications, 2007.

Falah, Ghazi-Walid, and Caroline Rose Nagel. *Geographies of Muslim Women: Gender, Religion, and Space.* New York: The Guilford Press, 2005.

Feng, Pin-chia. *The Female Bildungsroman by Toni Morrison and Maxine Hong Kingston: A Postmodern Reading.* New York: P. Lang, 1998.

Gall, Carlotta. "Afghan Motherhood in a Fight for Survival." *New York Times,* May 25, 2003. http://query.nytimes.com/gst/fullpage.html?res=9B00EED61531F936A15756C0A9659C8B63&sec=&spon=&partner=permalink&exprod=permalink (accessed May 26, 2008).

Gall, Timothy, and Gale Research Inc. *Worldmark Encyclopedia of Cultures and Daily Life.* Detroit: Gale, 1998.

Gauhari, Farooka. *An Afghan Woman's Odyssey.* Lincoln: University of Nebraska Press, 2004.

Ghafour, Hamida. *The Sleeping Buddha: The Story of Afghanistan through the Eyes of One Family.* Toronto: McArthur & Co., 2007.

Gross, Terry and Khaled Hosseini. "An Afghan Story: Khaled Hosseini and 'Kite Runner'" National Public Radio, *Fresh Air,* WHYY Radio, August 11, 2005. http://www.npr.org/templates/story/story.php?storyId=4795618 (accessed September 7, 2008).

Hansen, Liane, and Khaled Hosseini. "Khaled Hosseini Discusses His Childhood in Afghanistan and His Novel *The Kite Runner*." National Public Radio, *Weekend Edition Sunday*, July 27, 2003. http://www.npr.org/templates/story/story.php?storyId=1358775 (accessed July 7, 2008).

Harrell, John. *Origins and Early Traditions of Storytelling*. Kensington, CA: York House, 1983.

Horowitz, Rosemary. *Elie Wiesel and the Art of Storytelling*. Jefferson, NC: McFarland & Co., 2006.

Hosseini, Khaled. "Afghans Are Disenchanted and Fear Being Forgotten." *The Independent* (London, England), November 1, 2007. http://www.independent.co.uk/opinion/commentators/khaled-hosseini-afghans-are-disenchanted-and-fear-being-forgotten-398441.html (accessed May 4, 2009).

————. "Desperation in Kabul." *New York Times,* July 1, 2003. http://www.nytimes.com/2003/07/01/opinion/01HOSS.html?scp=1&sq=%22Desperation%20in%20Kabul%22%20&st=cse (accessed May 4, 2009).

————. "Journalism Is Not a Capital Crime." *Wall Street Journal,* February 1, 2008, sec. A-15.

————. "Khaled Hosseini: *A Thousand Splendid Suns*." Free Library Podcast. Free Library of Philadelphia, Recorded May 24, 2007. http://libwww.freelibrary.org/podcast/?podcastID=15 (accessed March 2, 2009).

————. Khaled Hosseini Blog. "Film Version of *A Thousand Splendid Suns*," March 31, 2008. http://khaledhosseini.com/blog/2008/03/film_version_of_a_thousand_spl.html (accessed October 28, 2008).

————. Khaled Hosseini Blog. "Hidden Treasures from Afghanistan," July 16, 2008. http://khaledhosseini.com/blog/2008/07/hidden_treasures_from_afghanis_1.html (accessed October 28, 2008).

————. Khaled Hosseini Blog. "New Primary School in Afghanistan," November 28, 2008. http://khaledhosseini.com/blog/2008/11/new_primary_school_in_northern_1.html (accessed May 4, 2009)

————. Khaled Hosseini Blog. "Optimism or Pessimism—Thoughts on Afghanistan's Future," October 11, 2008. http://khaledhosseini.com/blog/2008/10/optimism_or_pessimism_thoughts_1.html (accessed October 28, 2008).

————. Khaled Hosseini Official Web Site. http://khaledhosseini.com (accessed May 4, 2009).

————. Khaled Hosseini Official Web Site. "Discussion Videos." http://khaledhosseini.com/hosseini-bookgroupdiscussion.html (accessed May 4, 2009).

————."Khaled Hosseini on Writing." Amazon.com. http://www.amazon.com/gp/feature.html?ie=UTF8&docId=1000146431 (accessed September 7, 2008).

————. "McCain and Palin Are Playing with Fire." *Washington Post,* October 12, 2008, B-05 (accessed on January 22, 2009 through *Access World News*).

————. "Paperback Writer: Returning to Kabul Left Khaled Hosseini with a Sense of Déjà vu." *The Guardian,* December 18, 2004 (accessed on January 22, 2009 through *Access World News*).

————. "What Does $6,500 Buy? A Healthier, Happier Village." *New York Times* December 23, 2007. http://www.nytimes.com/2007/12/23/fashion/23hosseini.html (accessed May 4, 2009).

Hower, Edward. "The Servant." *The New York Times,* August 3, 2003, sec. 7, Book Review Desk.

Iacopino, Vincent, and Physicians for Human Rights (U.S.). *The Taliban's War on Women: A Health and Human Rights Crisis in Afghanistan: A Report.* Boston: Physicians for Human Rights, 1998.

IMDb. "The Kite Runner (2007)." IMDb: The Internet Movie Database. http://www.imdb.com/title/tt0419887/ (accessed November 6, 2008).

Jones, Tamara. "An Old, Familiar Face: Writer Khaled Hosseini, Lifting the Veil on Afghanistan." *Washington Post,* May 28, 2007, sec. C01.

Kakutani, Michiko. "A Woman's Lot in Kabul, Lower than a House Cat's." *New York Times,* May 29, 2007, sec. E, The Arts/Cultural Desk; Books of the Times.

Kirsch, Irwin S., U.S. Office of Educational Research and Improvement, Educational Testing Service, and National Center for Education Statistics. *Adult Literacy in America: A First Look at the Results of the National Adult Literacy Survey.* Washington, DC: Office of Educational Research and Improvement, U.S. Department of Education, 2002.

Korzon, David. "A Storyteller's Story: Khaled Hosseini and 'The Kite Runner.'" *The Village Rambler* (May-June 2005). http://villagerambler.com/issue_may05.html (accessed August 31, 2008).

Latifa. *My Forbidden Face: Growing Up Under the Taliban: A Young Woman's Story.* Written with Chékéba Hachemi. New York: Hyperion, 2001.

Levy, Reuben. *An Introduction to Persian Literature.* New York: Columbia University Press, 1969.

Maryles, Daisy. "Paperback Bestsellers/Trade." *Publishers Weekly* (July 28, 2008, and January 19, 2009).

McFadden, Cynthia. "'The Kite Runner'; Hollywood Scandal." *ABC News Transcript,* December 13, 2007 (accessed October 28, 2008 via *Lexis-Nexis Academic*).

McGillis, Ian. "Enduring Sorrow in Afghanistan; Hosseini's Second Novel Centres on the Lives of Two Women." *The Gazette* (Montreal), May 26, 2007, sec. Weekend: Books, J5.

Mehta, Sunita, ed. *Women for Afghan Women: Shattering Myths and Claiming the Future*. New York: Palgrave Macmillan, 2002.

Meo, Nick. "From Persecution to Adulation, the New Face of Afghan Cinema." *The Independent* (London, England), November 29, 2004. http://www.independent.co.uk/news/world/asia/from-persecution-to-adulation-the-new-face-of-afghan-cinema-534927.html (accessed May 5, 2009).

Milvy, Erika. "'The Kite Runner' Controversy." Salon.com, December 9, 2007. http://www.salon.com/ent/movies/feature/2007/12/09/hosseini/ (accessed September 7, 2008).

Monger, George. *Marriage Customs of the World: From Henna to Honeymoons*. Santa Barbara, CA: ABC-CLIO, 2004.

Mortenson, Greg, and David Oliver Relin, *Three Cups of Tea: One Man's Mission to Promote Peace . . . One School at a Time*. New York: Viking, 2006.

Mousavi, Sayed Askar. *The Hazaras of Afghanistan: An Historical, Cultural, Economic and Political Study*. New York: St. Martin's Press, 1997.

Mullen, Mark. "Dr. Khaled Hosseini, Author of 'The Kite Runner,' Discusses His Book." *Sunday Today*, NBC News, October 16, 2005 (accessed through LexisNexis Academic).

Naby, Eden. "The Afghan Diaspora: Reflections on the Imagined Country." In *Central Asia and the Caucasus: Transnationalism and Diaspora*, edited by Touraj Atabaki and Sanjyot Mehendale. New York: Routledge, 2005.

"Paperback Best Sellers." *New York Times Book Review* (January 18, 2009): 20.

Pazira, Nelofer. *A Bed of Red Flowers: In Search of My Afghanistan*. New York: Free Press, 2005.

Petronius. *The Satyricon*. Oxford: Clarendon Press, 1996.

Rais, Shah Muhammad. *Once Upon a Time There Was a Bookseller in Kabul*. Kabul, Afghanistan: Shah M Book Co., 2007.

Rasekh, Zora. "Public Health: A Reconstruction Priority in Afghanistan." In *Women for Afghan Women: Shattering Myths and Claiming the Future* by Sunita Mehta, ed. New York: Palgrave Macmillan, 2002.

Rodriguez, Deborah. *Kabul Beauty School: An American Woman Goes Behind the Veil*. New York: Random House, 2007

Roemer, Michael. *Telling Stories: Postmodernism and the Invalidation of Traditional Narrative*. Lanham, MD: Rowman & Littlefield, 1995.

Ruthchild, Rochelle Goldberg. "The End Is Far, and Time Is Short." *Women's Review of Books* 23, no. 6 (2006).

Sadat, Mir Hekmatullah. "The Afghan Experience: An Exploratory Study of Societal Realities Through the Lenses of Afghan Diasporic Literary Works." PhD diss., Claremont Graduate University and San Diego State University, 2006.

Sahar, David. "The Art of Gudiparan Bazi." *Afghana!* (afghana.com). Afghan Kite Discussion Forum, January 15, 2001. http://afghana.com/Entertainment/Gudiparanbazi.htm (accessed May 5, 2009).

Saikal, Amin, A. G. Ravan Farhadi, and Kirill Nourzhanov. *Modern Afghanistan: A History of Struggle and Survival.* New York: I.B. Tauris, 2004.

Sandstrom, Karen. "Book Review: Compelling Novel Follows a Coward to Kabul." *Newhouse News Service*, June 5, 2003 (accessed through *Lexis-Nexis Academic*).

Seierstad, Åsne. *The Bookseller of Kabul.* Boston: Little, Brown & Company, 2003.

Sethna, Razeshta. "Interview—Khaled Hosseini." *Newsline*, November 2003. http://www.newsline.com.pk/newsnov2003/newsbeat4nov.htm (accessed September 7, 2008).

Shakib, Siba. *Afghanistan, Where God Only Comes to Weep.* London: Century, 2002.

Skaine, Rosemarie. *The Women of Afghanistan Under the Taliban.* Jefferson, NC: McFarland, 2002.

Steele, Valerie. *Encyclopedia of Clothing and Fashion.* Scribner Library of Daily Life. Farmington Hills, MI: Charles Scribner's Sons, 2005.

Sterne, Laurence. *The Life and Opinions of Tristram Shandy, Gentleman.* 1760. New York: Oxford University Press, 1983.

Stewart, Rory. *The Places in Between.* Orlando, FL: Harcourt, 2006.

Steyn, Stefaan. "Afghan Struggle." *Herald Sun* (Australia), September 16, 2008. sec. Learn, 65.

Sultan, Masuda. *My War at Home.* New York: Washington Square Press, 2006.

"Taliban: No Subversive Gateaux: As Titanic Fever Grips Kabul, Hardline Militia Proves No Match for . . . Iced Cakes." *The Guardian* (London, England) November 24, 2000 (accessed online January 19, 2009, through *Access World News*).

Tonkin, Boyd. "Is the Arab World Ready for a Literary Revolution?" *The Independent* (London, England), April 15, 2008, sec. Books. http://www.independent.co.uk/arts-entertainment/books/features/is-the-arab-world-ready-for-a-literary-revolution-808946.html (accessed May 5, 2009).

United Nations Statistics Division. "Gender Info 2007." http://data.un.org/Data.aspx?q=afghanistan+adult+literacy&d=GenderStat&f=inID:49;crID:84&c=1,2,3,4,5,6&s=_crEngNameOrderBy:asc,timeID:desc&v=1 (accessed January 22, 2009).

United Nations Statistics Division. "Key Global Indicators, Infant Mortality, Afghanistan 1960–2005." http://data.un.org/Data.aspx?q=afghanistan+infant+mortality&d=CDB&f=srID:1230;crID:4&c=2,3,4&s=_crEngNameOrderBy:asc,yr:desc&v=1l (accessed January 22, 2009).

United Nations Statistics Division. "Millennium Development Goals Database, Maternal Mortality, Afghanistan 2005." http://data.un.org/Data.aspx? q=afghanistan+maternal+mortality&d=MDG&f=seriesRowID:553;country ID:4&c=2,3,4&s=_countryEnglishNameOrderBy:asc,year:desc&v=1

Vick, Tom. *Asian Cinema: A Field Guide*. New York: Collins, 2007.

Weich, Dave. "Powells.com Interviews—Khaled Hosseini's Splendid Second Act." Powell's Books, July 12, 2007. http://www.powells.com/authors/ khaledhosseini.html (accessed September 7, 2008).

Whitlock, Gillian. "The Skin of the Burqa: Recent Life Narratives from Afghanistan." *Biography: An Interdisciplinary Quarterly* 28, no. 1 (2005): 54–76.

World Bank. *World Development Indicators*. Washington, DC: World Bank, 2007. http://www.worldbank.org.

Zoya. *Zoya's Story: An Afghan Woman's Struggle for Freedom*. Written with John Follain and Rita Cristofari. New York: William Morrow, 2002.

# INDEX

Ansari, Aabdullah, 21. *See also* poets

Abdalla, Khalid, 89, 97. *See also The Kite Runner*, the film

Afghan diaspora, 8; Hosseini, 2, 7, 81; in *The Kite Runner*, 7, 17, 19, 22, 26, 30, 31, 35; in literature, 3 (*see also* diaspora); Little Kabul, 8; in San Francisco Bay Area, 2; in *A Thousand Splendid Suns*, 51; on the Web, 98, 100, 101

Afghan immigrant community. *See* Afghan diaspora

Afghan Minister of Women's Affairs, 90

Afghanistan: Buddhas of Bamiyan, 55, 60; coups, 1, 2, 7, 28, 76, 84, 112, 114; drought, 8, 51; Hazaras, 42, 75; history, 58–60, 67, 84, 100, 101, 109, 110, 115, 116; Islamic State of, 51; languages, 6, 22, 62, 75, 76; laws concerning women, 50, 53, 62, 70, 72; literature, 60; Mujahideen, 59; Panjshir, 50; population, 27, 48, 55, 68, 75, 112; Republic of, 7; U. S. invasion of, 20, 27, 54, 65, 66, 80–84, 87, 90, 110, 115; wars, 67; women, 69, 110, 111, 113, 114

Afghanistan, ethnic groups and minorities, 6, 27, 70, 71, 73, 74, 76, 77; Hosseini's views on, 5, 106; in

*The Kite Runner*, 27, 36, 37, 39, 41, 42. *See also* Hazaras

Akbar, Said Hyder, 83, 84, 107, 108, 113, 114

Amanullah, King, 58, 75

Amazon.com, 3

Amir, character in *The Kite Runner*, 8, 36–44; with bullies, 28; flea market (*see also* flea market), 30, 31, 36, 44; guilt, 15, 29, 38, 42, 43; as immigrant, 6, 7, 17, 19, 22, 30, 31, 36; kite flying, 28, love of Westerns, 5; in Pakistan, 19, 32, 35; the phone call, 26, 32, 35; quest, 15, 16, 18, 19; rape of Hassan, 28, 29; relationship with father, 6, 7, 17, 22, 27, 28, 30, 32, 38; relationship with Hassan, 15, 17, 19, 26–29, 74; relationship with Soraya, 19, 26, 30, 40; rescue of Sohrab, 20, 32–34; return to Afghanistan, 32, 35; similarities to Hosseini, 3, 6, 99; as writer, 19, 32

Ansary, Mir Tamim, 2, 83, 84, 86, 96, 101, 110, 114

Arababshirali, Afghanistan, 81

Assef, character in *The Kite Runner*, 28, 37, 39, 43, 76; compared to Hitler, 76; rape of Hassan, 29, 42; as metaphor, 33; as Talib officer, 33, 42

Austen, Jane, 11, 12, 20

**About the Author**

REBECCA STUHR is an Associate Professor and Collection Development Librarian at Grinnell College.